A STRAIGHTFORWARD

GUIDE TO

PROBATE
AND THE LAW

Julie Peters

Straightforward Guides
www.straightforwardco.co.uk

© Straightforward Publishing 2010

British cataloguing in Publication Data. A catalogue record is available for this book from the British library.

ISBN 9781847161512

Printed by GN Digital Press Essex
Cover design by Bookworks Islington

Whilst every effort has been taken to ensure that the information in this book is accurate at the time of going to press, the author and publisher recognise that the information can become out of date. This is particularly relevant to legal and tax information. The book is therefore sold on the understanding that no responsibility for errors and omissions is assumed and no responsibility is held for the information held within.

CONTENTS

Introduction

PART TWO – OBTAINING PROBATE AND ADMINISTERING ESTATES

Introduction

This brief book is intended for the person who wishes to understand the law as it affects probate and also the basic principles behind producing a will. It will benefit those who wish to proceed to probate without a solicitor and who wish to understand the finer points of the law as it affects a last will and testament. It will also be suitable for the person who wishes to use a solicitor but wants to understand more generally.

The book is structured so that, in the first section, all the important elements of the production of a will are laid out with all the important points covered. General points are outlined along with the reasons for making a will. The actual production of a will is covered and a sample will is drawn up.

In addition, taxation issues are covered, along with the role of the courts. Wills and probate in Scotland is also covered.

The second section of the book deals in depth with the grant of probate and also letters of administration. This is followed by an examination of the distribution of estates and the role of the executor.

Contemplating one's will is not the most cheerful of subjects but it is absolutely essential that every person has a last will and testament produced long before their death. Understanding the meaning and nature of probate and wills is essential in order to ensure that a persons estate is administered effectively after their death.

1

Probate Generally

Probate simply means that the executor's powers to administer the estate of a dead person have been officially confirmed. A document called a "Grant of Representation" is given which enables those administering the estate to gain access to all relevant information, financial or otherwise concerning the person's estate.

Although anyone charged under a will to act on behalf of the dead persons estate has automatic authority to represent, there are certain cases where evidence of probate is required. If no will exists or no executors have been appointed, then it will be necessary to obtain "Letters of administration" which involves a similar procedure.

Under common law, probate has a number of objectives. These are:

- To safeguard creditors of the deceased

- To ensure reasonable provision is made for the deceased's dependants

- To distribute the balance of the estate in accordance with the intentions of the person whose will it is.

One of the key factors affecting the need to obtain probate is how much money is involved under the terms of a will. Where the sums involved are relatively small then financial institutions and other organisations will not normally want to see evidence of probate. However, it should be remembered that no one is obliged to release anything relating to a dead persons estate unless letters of administration or documents of probate can be shown. Those responsible for administering the estate must find out from the organisations concerned what the necessary procedure is.

Applying for probate

Where a will is in existence and executors have been appointed then any one of the named people can make the application. Where a will is in existence but no executors have been appointed, then the person who benefits from the whole estate should make the application. This would be the case where any known executor cannot or will not apply for probate.

Where there is no will in existence then the next of kin can apply for probate. There is an order of priority relating to the application:

- The surviving spouse

- A child of the deceased

- A parent of the deceased

- A brother or sister of the deceased

- Another relative of the deceased

The person applying for probate must be over eighteen. 'Children' includes any that are illegitimate. If a child dies before the deceased then one of his or her children can apply for probate.

Application for probate

This can be done through any probate registry or office. There is usually one in every main town and any office in any area will accept the application. If you are writing then you should always address your correspondence to a registry and not an office. You can also contact the Probate Personal Application Department at the Probate Registry. See 'Useful Addresses' at the back of this book.

Before discussing probate and general administration of a deceased person's estate, which is outlined in part 2 of this book, we will first look at the processes involved in the production of a will. It is essential that this all-important area is understood, both by the person making the will and also the executor of the estate.

2

Producing a Will-General Points

The main principle underlying any will is that, if you have possessions, or any other assets, then you need to organise a will which will ensure that chosen people benefit after your death.

In the majority of cases, a persons affairs are relatively uncomplicated and should not involve the use of a solicitor.

There are certain basic rules to be followed in the formation of a will and if they are then it should be legally binding.

The only inhibiting factor on the disposal of your assets will be any tax liability following death, which will be dealt with later in this book. There are a number of other factors to consider, however:

- Age of person making a will

A will made by anyone under the age of eighteen, known as a minor, will not be valid unless that person is a member of the services (armed forces) and is on active service.

- Mental health considerations

A will formed by a person, who was insane at the time of writing, will not be valid. Mental illness in itself is not a barrier to creating a will, as long as proof can be shown that the person was not insane at the time of writing. Subsequent mental illness, following the formation of a will, will not be a barrier to a will's validity.

- Definition of insanity

Insanity, or this particular condition, will normally apply to anyone certified as such and detained in a mental institution. In addition, the Mental Health Act covers those in " a state of arrested or incomplete development of mind which includes sub-normality of intelligence and is of such a nature or degree that the patient is incapable of living an independent life or guarding against serious exploitation.

In any situation where there is doubt as to a persons capabilities then it is always best to have any will validated by an expert. This applies to anyone, not just those classified as insane.

The main point of any will is that, in the final analysis, a court would have to be satisfied that the contents of the will are genuine, there has not been any attempt whatsoever to alter the contents or to influence that persons mind. The person writing the will must have fashioned its contents with no outside interference.

Unfortunately, the history of the production of people's last will and testament is littered with greedy and unscrupulous persons who wish to gain from another's demise. It is necessary to be careful!

3
The Reasons for Making
A Will

The main reason for making a will is to ensure that you make the choice as to who you leave your possessions, and not the state. You can also impose any specific conditions you want in your will. For example, you can impose age conditions or conditions relating to the need to perform certain duties before benefiting.

If you do not make a will then, on your death, the law of intestacy will apply to the disposal of your estate. You will have had no say and certain criteria are applied by the state, which will take responsibility.

In the circumstances described above, after costs such as funeral and administration of other aspects of death, an order of preference is established, as follows:

- Your spouse, which is your husband or wife

- Any children you may have. This includes all children, whether by marriage, illegitimate or adopted.

- Parents

- Brothers and sisters

- Half brothers or sisters

- Grandparents

- Uncles and aunts

- Uncles and aunts (half blood)

It is the law of intestacy that if any of the above, in that order, die before the person who is the subject of intestacy, then their children will automatically benefit in their place.

There are conditions which will affect the above order of beneficiaries:

- If the spouse of a person is still living and there are no surviving children, parents, brothers or sisters or any of their offspring living then the spouse will benefit solely

- If the spouse is still living and there is children, the estate will be divided along the following lines:

The spouse will take all the personal items and up to £75,000 if money is involved. This will be augmented by interest on the money from the date of death. There will be a life interest in half of the residue of the estate. This means use as opposed to ownership. In the case of money it relates to interest on capital only and not the capital itself;

Children (equal shares) Half the residue of the estate plus the other half on the death of the spouse.

If the spouse is still alive, there are no children but there are other relatives, such as parents, brothers and sisters and their children the following rules apply:

The spouse will have all the personal items and up to £125000 if it is available, interest on money and half the residue of the estate;

Parents will receive half the residue or, if there are no parents alive then brothers and sisters will, in equal shares, keep half the residue.

By law, the spouse is entitled to carry on living in the matrimonial home after death. The matrimonial home is defined as the place where he or she had been living at the time of death.

If there is no spouse living but there are children then the estate will be divided equally between them. This will occur when they are over the age of eighteen or marry, whichever occurs first.

If there is no spouse and no children but there are parents, then the estate will be divided equally between them. If there is no spouse, no children and no parents, then the estate will be divided equally between brothers and sisters. If there are no brothers and sisters then half brothers and sisters. If none, grandparents. If not, uncles and aunts and if none to half blood uncles and aunts.

As can be seen, the law of intestacy tries to ensure that at least someone benefits from a person's possessions on death. There is a ranking order and in most cases there would be someone to benefit. There are certain categories of person who fall outside of the law of intestacy, even though there may have been some connection in the past:

Divorced and separated persons

There is no right of entitlement whatsoever for a divorced person to benefit from an estate on death. This right ceases from the decree absolute.

If a separation order is granted by a divorce court then there is no entitlement to benefit. If the separation is informal and there is separate habitation or a Magistrates court order has been granted for separation then there is normal entitlement.

Cohabitation

The law of intestacy dictates that, if you were living with someone, but not married, at the time of death, then that person has no direct claim to the estate. However, in practice this operates somewhat differently and there is a law, Provision for Family and Dependants Act 1975 under which cohabitees can claim. We will be discussing this a little later.

Although anyone has a right to have their estate distributed in accordance with the law of intestacy it is highly inadvisable. It is better at all time to ensure that you have complete control over where your money goes. It may be that you do not wish immediate family to benefit over others and that you wish to leave all your money to a particular favoured person or to an institution. This can only be achieved by personalising your will and remaining in control of what happens after your death.

4

The Decision When to Produce a Will

It is essential that you make a will as soon as possible. If you leave it, there is a chance that you may never get round to doing it and may be reliant upon the state doing it for you. There is also the chance that you will leave a situation where people start to contest your possessions, fight amongst each other and fall out.

There are many things to consider when you decide to produce a will. As a person gets older, chances are that he or she will become wealthier. Savings grow, endowments increase, insurance policies become more valuable, property is purchased and so on. A bank balance in itself is no indicator of worth, as there are many other elements which add up to wealth.

Changes in personal circumstances often justify the need to make a will.

- Ownership of property

- Children

- Marriage or remarriage

- Employment

- Illness

- Divorce and separation

- Increase in personal wealth, such as an inheritance

Ownership of property

Ownership of property usually implies a mortgage. If you are wise it will also imply life insurance to at least the value of the property. It is very prudent to make a will which specifies exactly to whom the property will be left. As we have seen, the law of intestacy provides for the decision if you do not have a will.

Children

As we have seen, under the law of intestacy, any children you have will benefit after your death. However, it is very sensible, under a will, to specify how and when they will benefit. It could be that you may let someone else make that decision later on. Whatever, you should make it very clear in your will.

Marriage or remarriage

The most important point to remember is that marriage or remarriage will automatically revoke the provisions of any former will, although this is not the case in Scotland. Therefore, when marrying you should make certain that your will is up to date and that you have altered the provisions. In short, you should amend your will, or produce a new will in order to outline clearly what you want your new partner to have.

Employment

You should be very aware that certain types of employment carry greater risks than others. This will necessitate producing a will as soon as possible as if you are in a high-risk category then you need to ensure that those nearest you are catered for.

Illness

Illness is something that none of us want but cannot avoid if it decides to strike. No matter how healthy you are you should take this into account when considering putting together a will. In addition, some people have a family history of illness and chances are that they too could suffer. Therefore illness is a very real motivator for producing a will.

Divorce and separation

The law of intestacy states that if you die your divorced spouse loses all rights to your estate. You may not want this to happen and make provisions in your will. Although children of any marriage will benefit it could be that you may wish to make slightly different provisions for different children.

Increase in personal wealth

Financial success, and inheritance will increase your wealth and inevitably make you estate more complicated. It is absolutely essential to ensure that you have a will and that you are updating that will regularly to take into account increased assets.

The provisions of a will

Having considered some of the many reasons for producing a will, it is now necessary to look at exactly what goes into a will.

Essentially, the purpose of a will is to ensure that everything you have accumulated in your life is disposed of in accordance with your own desires. The main areas to consider when formulating a will are:

- Money you have saved, in whatever form

- Any buildings (property) you have

- Any land you have

- Any insurance policies you have. This is of utmost importance

- Any shares you may own

- Trusts set up

- Any other personal effects

Money you have saved

Money is treated as part of your wider estate and will automatically go to those named as the main beneficiaries. However, you might wish to make individual bequests to other people outside your family. These have to be specified. When including any provisions in your will relating to money, you should be very clear about the whereabouts of any saving accounts or endowments, premium bonds etc. Life becomes very difficult if you have left sums of money but there is no knowledge of the whereabouts of this. Inevitably, solicitors have to be employed and this becomes very expensive indeed.

Property

It is necessary to make provisions for any property you have. If you are the sole owner of a property then you can dispose of it as you wish. Any organisation with a superior interest would take an interest, particularly if there are mortgages outstanding. It is important to remember that if you are a joint owner of a property, such as a joint tenancy, then on death this joint ownership reverts to the other joint owner, bringing it into sole ownership. Leasehold property can be different only in so much as the executor of an estate will usually need permission before assigning a lease. This can be obtained from the freeholder.

Land

Although the same principles apply to land as to property, indeed often the two are combined, in certain circumstances land may be owned separately. In this case the land and everything on it can be left in the will.

Insurance policies

The contents of any insurance policy needs to be checked carefully. In certain cases there are restrictions on who can benefit on death. Particular people may be specified and you have no alternative but to let such people benefit, even though your own circumstances may have changed. If there are no restrictions then you can bequeath any money as you see fit.

Shares and trusts

Shares can normally be bequeathed in a will as anything else. However, depending on the type of share, it is just possible that there may be restrictions. One such situation is where shares are held in a private company and there may be a buy back clause.

Trusts can be set up for the benefit of family and friends. However, a trust, by its very nature is complex as the law dealing with trusts is complex. It is absolutely essential, if you are considering setting up a trust to get specialist advice.

Personal effects

Although you are perfectly entitled to leave specific items of personal effects in your will, such legacies are separate from those of other possessions such as money or land. The law recognises that in some cases there may not be enough money to pay expenses related to your death. Any money owed will be retrieved from any financial gifts you have outlined. However, personal effects cannot be touched if you have clearly identified these in your will. This includes items of value such as jewelry. It is not enough to be general on this point. You must specify exactly what it is you are leaving and to whom. Remember, certain gifts will be taxable. We will be covering this later.

The funeral

It is common practice to include such matters as how you wish to be buried, in what manner and the nature of the ceremony, in your will. You should discuss these arrangements with your next of kin in addition to specifying them in your will as arrangements may be made for a funeral before details of a will are made public. Another way is to detail your wishes in a letter and pass this on to your executor to ensure that the details are known beforehand.

There is no reason why any of your instructions should not be carried out, subject to the law. However, your executor can override your wishes if necessary and expedient.

You can, in addition, make known your wishes for maintenance of your grave after your death. Agreement of the local authority, or relevant burial authority must be sought and there is no obligation on them to do this. In addition, there is a time limit of 99 years in force.

The use of your body after death

It could be that you have decided to leave your body for medical research or donate your organs. This can be done during your final illness, in writing or in front of a minimum of two witnesses. You should contact your local hospital or General Practitioner about this, they will supply you with more details.

Making a recital

A recital consists of a statement at the end of your will which explains how and why you have drawn up a will in the way you have. This is not commonly done but sometimes may be necessary, especially if you have cut people out of your will but do not intend to cause confusion or hurt.

Recitals are sometimes necessary in order to clarify a transfer of authority to others on your death. This could be in business for example. In addition, you may wish to recognise someone's contribution to your life, for example a long serving employee or a particular friend.

5

Making Provisions In Your Will

Who to name

When including persons, or organisations, in your will it is better to form a separate list right at the outset.

Naming individuals in your will

There are certain criteria which apply when naming individuals in a will, although in principle you can name who you want. Any person considered an adult, i.e. over 18, can benefit from your will. However, if a person cannot be traced within a time period of seven years after being named, or dies before you, then the amount left in your will to that person is included in what is known as the residue of your estate, what is left after all bequests. You can also make a bequest in your will to cover that eventuality, that is for another named person to benefit in his or her place.

If the bequest is to your own children or any other direct descendant and they die before you then the gift will automatically go to their children, unless there is something to the contrary in your will. In addition, if you make a gift to two or more people and one dies then that share is automatically passed to the other (joint owner).

Children

You are entitled to leave what you want in your will to children whether they are illegitimate or stepchildren. Stepchildren should be stipulated in your will. If children are under 18 then it will be probably necessary to leave property such as land, in trust for them until they reach 18 or any other age stated in the will. No child under 18 can be a trustee.

Those people who are not British citizens, i.e. foreigners can benefit from your will in the same way as anyone else. The only real restriction to this is if there is a state of war between your own country and theirs, in which case it will be necessary to wait until peace is declared.

Mental illness

There is nothing currently in law which prevents a person suffering mental illness from receiving a bequest under a will. Obviously, depending on the state of mind of that person it could be that someone may have to accept the gift and take care of it on the person's behalf.

Bankruptcy

If a person is either bankrupt or facing bankruptcy then if that person receives a gift there is a chance that it could end up in the hands of a creditor.

To avoid this happening you can establish a protective trust which will enable the person in receipt of the gift to enjoy any interest arising from the gift during a specific time.

Animals

It is possible to leave money to animals for their care and well being. There is a time limit involved for receipt of the money, which is currently a period of 21 years.

Groups

There is no problem legally with leaving money and other gifts to groups or organisations. However, it is necessary to ensure that the wording of the will is structured in a certain way. It is necessary to understand some of the legislation concerning charities, in order that your bequest can be deemed charitable.

Leaving money/gifts to charities

Many people leave bequests to charity. Major charities often give advice to individuals and other organisations on how to do that. Smaller charities can pose a problem as they may not be as sound and as well administered as larger ones. It is best to stipulate an alternative charity in the event of the smaller one ceasing to operate. If for whatever reason you bequest cannot be passed on to the group concerned then it will be left in the residue of your estate and could be liable to tax. There are a number of causes which might be deemed as charitable. These are:

- Educational causes
- Help for the community
- Animal welfare
- Help for the elderly
- Disabled
- Religious groups
- Sick, such as hospices

In the event of making a bequest to a charitable cause, it is certain that you will need expert advice, as with the setting up of trusts.

6

Writing a Will

The writing of a will and the way you word it, is of the utmost importance and it is here that skill is needed. If you word the will wrongly then it can be contested, rejected and your estate could be administered by the state.

As long as you observe certain rules then there is no reason why you should go wrong, however.

One of the key rules is that there should be nothing in your will that can be ambiguous or open to interpretation. It is essential to ensure that your intentions are crystal clear. It will probably be necessary to get someone else to look at your will to ensure that it is understood by others.

Preparation of will

A will can of course be rewritten. However, it is very important indeed to ensure that you have spent enough time in the initial preparation stages of your will as it could be enacted at any time, in the event of sudden death. If your possessions are numerous then it is highly likely that the preparation stage will be fairly lengthy as the dividing up will take more thought. This gets more complicated depending on your other circumstances, such as whether you are married or single, have children, intend to leave money to organizations, etc.

You need to make a clear list of what it is you have in order to be able to achieve clarity in your will. For example, property and other possessions will take in any buildings and land you own plus money in various accounts or other forms of saving. In addition there could be jewelry and other valuables to take into account. It is necessary to quantify the current value of these possessions. It is also necessary to balance this out by making a list of any outstanding loans/mortgages or other debts you may have. Funeral costs should come into this. It is essential that you do not attempt to give away more than you actually have and also to deduce any tax liabilities from the final amount after debts. The wording of any will is always done with tax liability in mind.

Listing those who will benefit from your will

Making a list of beneficiaries is obviously necessary, including all groups, individuals and others who will benefit. With each beneficiary you should list exactly what it is that you bequeath. If a trust is necessary, then note this and note down the name of proposed trustees. These persons should be in agreement before being named. Contact any charities that will benefit. They can supply you with a legacy clause to include in your will.

The most important point, at this stage, is that you ensure that what you are leaving does not exceed the estate and that, if liable for tax, then there is sufficient left over to meet these liability.

Make a note of any recitals that you wish to include in your will and exactly what you wish to say.

The choice of an executor of your will

The job of any executor is to ensure that your will is administered in accordance with the terms therein as far as is legally possible at that time. It is absolutely essential to ask those people is they consent to being an executor. They may well refuse which could pose problems. You can ask friends or family or alternatively you can ask a solicitor or your bank. They will make a charge for this. However, they are much less likely to make a mistake in the execution of the will than an untrained individual. They will charge and this should be provided for.

If you do choose to appoint an untrained executor, then it is good policy to appoint at least two in order to ensure that there is an element of double-checking and that there are enough people to fulfill the required duties.

The presentation of your will

You can either prepare your will on ordinary sheets of paper or used specially prepared forms which can be obtained from stationers or book shops. Bookshops will usually sell "will packs" which take you through the whole preparation stage, from contemplation to completion. Try to avoid handwriting your will. If it cannot be read then it will be invalid. You should always try to produce it on a word processor or typewriter. This can be more easily altered at any time.

The advantage of using a pre-printed form is that it has all of the required phrases on it and you just fill in the blanks. It just may be that you are not in the position to write your will, as you may be one of the considerable numbers of people who cannot read or write in this country. In this case, you can get someone else to write it for you although it is essential that you understand the contents. Get someone else, independent of the person who wrote it to read it back to you to ensure that the contents reflect your wishes.

The Wording of a will

The wording of a will is of the utmost importance as it is absolutely necessary to ensure that you produce a clear document which is an instrument of your own will. The following are some words, which appear in wills, with an explanation of their precise meaning and pitfalls:

"Beneficiary"

this means someone or something that benefits as a result of a gift in a will.

"Bequeath"

"I bequeath" in a will usually refers to personal property such as personal property and money.

"Children"

this includes both legitimate and illegitimate children and also adopted children. Where a gift is to a child and that child has children and dies before the death of the person making the will then the gift will pass on to the child or children of that child if they are living at the time of the testators death unless an intention to the contrary appears in the will. "Children" does not usually include stepchildren and if you wish a stepchild to be included then this will need to be specified. Children will include stepchildren where there are only step children alive at the time of making the will.

"Children" can also include grandchildren where it is clear that this was intended or there are only grandchildren and no other children are alive at the date of making a will. You should always specify grandchildren when you want them included.

"Descendants" this means children, grandchildren, great grandchildren and so on down the line. A gift using this word is sometimes phrased "to my descendants living at my death" which includes all those who are alive at the time of the death of the person making a will. Male descendants means males who are descended from females as well as those who are descended from males. A gift to descendants means that they all take equal shares. If you wish each merely to take in default of a parent or parents (e.g. if a parent predeceases you) then add the words "per stirpes".

"Devise"

"I devise" in a will usually refers to a gift of land, which includes a house.

"Executor/Executrix"

this is the person or persons you appoint to administer your will and to carry out your wishes as expressed in your will. Anyone can be appointed an executor, usually expressed as a clause in your will. The few exceptions are those of a minor and those of unsound mind. Solicitors and banks can also be appointed.

Executors can also receive gifts under the will. The executor cannot charge fees, banks and solicitors do but the will must stipulate this. Because of the fact that executors can change their minds about taking on the task of administering your will, it is often better to have two.

"Family"

this word should not be used if it can be helped as it has been interpreted in several different ways. It is, by and large, far to general.

"Husband"

this means the husband at the time of making the will. In the event of a divorce, a person remains married until the decree absolute has been granted. Divorce alters the will in so far as any appointment of a former spouse as an executor becomes void, as do any bequests to that person, unless there is a contrary intention in the will.

Generally, if a marriage splits up it is best to review the provisions of a will.

"Infant"

this means a child under the age of eighteen. Land is given to trustees (usually) if left to those under eighteen, as an infanr cannot hold an estate in land.

"Issue"

this means all descendants but has been interpreted as having several meanings. In a simple will its use should be avoided altogether as again, it is far too general.

"Minor"

this has the same meaning as infant.

"Nephews"

the meaning of this term depends upon the context of the will. It is far safer, in any such general situation to be specific and name names.

"Next of kin"

this means the closest blood relation.

"Nieces"

the same applies as for nephews.

"Pecuniary legacy"

this means a gift of money in a will.

"Residue"

this means the amount that is left of your estate after effect has been given to all the gifts in your will and testamentary and other expenses have been paid.

"Survivor"

this may apply to persons who are not born at the time of the will. Therefore, a gift to all those who survive a person leaving the will could include all brothers and sisters not yet born.

"Testamentary expenses"

in a will the residue of an estate may be left to a person after all expenses. This includes all known expenses, such as the costs of administering the will.

"Trustee"

a trustee is someone entrusted to look after property for another until a certain age is attained or condition fulfilled. There should always be more than one trustee with two being a usual number.

"Wife"

this means the wife at the time of making the will. Again, in the event of a divorce, then the decree absolute must be granted before that person ceases to be a wife.

Safekeeping of a will

A will must always be kept safe and should be able to be located at the time of your death. You may spend a great deal of time on your will. However, if it cannot be found then it will be assumed that you have not made one. It is best practice to deposit the will with your or your family solicitor.

7
The Contents Of the Will

When writing a will, there is a recognised format which must be followed for the will to be deemed legal. The following constitutes the basic outline:

- A will states that this is your last will and testament
- Your full name and address must be on the will and the date of the will
- All previous wills, if they exist, must be revoked in writing
- There must be an appointment and payment of executors
- Provision for the appointment of a firm of solicitors, if appropriate
- The method of disposal of your body, whether by cremation or burial or whether you have chosen to leave your body for medical purposes. This is not essential
- Payment of testamentary expenses
- Payment of inheritance tax if you are giving gifts free of tax
- Any recital, e.g. any statement of affection or other which you wish to pass
- A list of specific items to be left in your will
- A list of all pecuniary legacies, headed "I give and bequeath the following pecuniary legacies"
- A list of all gifts of land headed "I give and devise"

- A clause dealing with the residue of your estate, such as any property and money remaining after all the gifts and payments of expenses in your will have been made
- Your usual signature
- The signature of two witnesses, neither of whom or whose spouses are given any gift in the will. There should be a statement that they were both present at the same time and either saw you making your signature or acknowledging that the signature is yours.

Making a list of the key steps to be taken when preparing a will
It is essential, before beginning to draft out your will to follow a check list of the key steps to be taken:

- Make a complete list of all property that you own, including any future property. Deduct any mortgages or loans in order to arrive at a figure which can be left in your will, or a net worth
- Next, make a list of all those people who will benefit under your will (beneficiaries)
- Note any expressions of affection that you want to make in your will
- Organise your executors. As we have seen, these can be members of your family, a bank, solicitor etc. You need to know the fees involved if you are using a professional practice. These should be allowed for in the will. Likewise, you may wish to leave something to those who act as executors for you
- Prepare your will, preferably typewritten on quality paper
- Make a list of all bequests of your goods that you wish to leave and a list of all the legacies of the money that you wish to leave

- Think about any specific beneficiaries and what this involves, such as a charity. Do you need to contact them and ask for their number or to enlist any help that they may give? Likewise, you may want to leave money to a pet. You will probably need advice on this
- Consider whether you want to create any trusts. Again, you will need advice concerning these
- Make sure that witnesses have signed your will
- Ensure that your signature is your usual one
- Make sure that the will is dated the day that it is signed.

- Fold up your will, place into an envelope and mark it "The last will and testament of_____ (add your name)

- Put your will in a safe place and tell your executors and next of kin where it is kept
- Remember to alter your will as your circumstances change. Destroy any old copies of wills.

The Thirty-day clause

If your immediate beneficiary dies within days of your own demise, unlikely but not unknown, the situation may well arise where the gifts left by you will pass elsewhere. To prevent this happening, you can make provision in your will stipulating another beneficiary should the immediate beneficiary not survive you by thirty days.

The use of a statutory will form

Statutory will forms are very helpful in that they have the necessary forms of words, in many cases. There are a number of forms. Form 2 for example, allows you to give all your possessions to someone without having to identify each possession. There are a number of other forms catering for different situations. One such form is form 4 which is designed for charitable bequests.

International wills

A provision now exists which is designed to aid those people who have property in a number of different countries. They can now make one will and have it administered in any country which is party to the convention. This can be done regardless of where the will was drawn up or where the assets are. There are a certain number of criteria to be followed, however:

- The will must be in writing. It can be in any language
- The person whose will it is must declare in front of a solicitor/notary that the will is really his or hers and this must be witnessed by two people
- The person making the will must then sign it at the end, and sign and number each page, in the presence of a solicitor and witnesses who must sign at the end. The date must be added, by a solicitor and a certificate must be attached, which should include details of where the will is kept.

It will be necessary to seek advice regarding international wills as they have only recently been introduced.

Sample Last Will and Testament

This is the last Will and Testament

Of me_____ of (address)_____

Made this_____ day of_____2010

1. I hereby revoke all former wills and testamentary dispositions heretofore made by me.

2. I appoint (executors and trustees) (hereinafter called "my trustees" which expression where the context admits includes any trustee or trustees hereof for the time being whether original or substituted) to be the executors and trustees thereof and I declare that any of my trustees being a solicitor or other profession shall be entitled to charge accordingly.

3. I appoint_____

4. Of_____

To be the guardian after the death of my wife husband_____ of any of my children who may then be minors.

4. If my wife or husband survives me by thirty days (but not otherwise) I give to him or her absolutely (Subject to payment of debts and other expenses) all my estate both real and personal whatsoever and wheresoever not hereby or by any codicil hereto otherwise specifically disposed of.

5. If my wife or husband as stated in this will is not living at my death the following provisions shall have effect:

I give all my estate both real and personal whatsoever and wheresoever not hereby or any codicil hereto otherwise specifically disposed of unto my trustees UPON TRUST to raise and discharge my debts and funeral and testamentary expenses and all legacies given hereby or by any codicil hereto and any and all taxes payable by reason of my death in respect of property given free of tax and subject thereto UPON TRUST to pay and divide the same equally between my children

_____Name

_____Address

And_____Of

_____

as shall survive me and attain the age of 18 years provided always that if any child of mine shall die before reaching 18 yrs or marry under that age leaving a child or children such last such last mentioned child or children shall take by substitution and if more than one in equal shares the share of my estate which his or her or their parent would have taken if he or she had survived me.

6. If neither my wife/husband nor children nor any of their issue are living at my death then I give all my estate, both real and personal whatsoever and wheresoever unto my trustees upon trust to raise and discharge thereout my debts and funeral and testamentary expenses and all legacies given hereby or by any codicil hereto and any and all taxes payable by reason of my death in respect of property given free of tax, and subject thereto UPON TRUST to pay and divide the same equally between:

_____Names

of_____Address

7. My Trustees shall have the following powers in addition to their general law powers:

a) to apply for the benefit of any beneficiary as my trustees think fit the whole or any part of the income from that part of my estate to which he is entitled or may in future be entitled.

b) to apply for the benefit of any beneficiary as my trustee thinks fit the whole or any part of the capital to which that beneficiary is entitled.

c) to exercise the power of appropriation conferred by section 41 of The Administration of Estates Act 1925 without obtaining any of the consents required by that section even though one or more of them may be beneficially interested.

d) to invest trust money and transpose investment with the same full and unrestricted freedom in their choice of investments as if they were an absolute beneficial owner and to apply trust money at any time and from time to time in the purchase with vacant possession or in the improvement of any freehold or leasehold house and to permit the same to be used by any person or person having an interest or prospective interest in my residuary estate upon such terms and conditions from time to time as my trustees in their absolute discretion may think fit.

e) To insure from loss or damage from fire or any other risk any property for the time being comprised in my residuary estate to any amount and even though a person is absolutely entitled to the property and to pay all premiums as due and any insurances out of the income or capital of my residuary estate.

8. I wish my body to be
buried_____

In witness to this document I set my hand this _____day of_____2010

Signed by said witness_____Name

Signature_____

8

The Intervention Of The Courts

Courts have wide powers to make alterations to a persons will, after that person's death. It can exercise these powers if the will fails to achieve the intentions of the person who wrote it, as a result of a clerical error or a failure to understand the instructions of the person producing the will. In addition, if mental illness can be demonstrated at the time of producing the will then this can also lead to the courts intervening.

In order to get the courts to exercise their powers, an application must be made within six months of the date on which probate is taken out. If gifts or other are distributed and a court order is made to rectify the will then all must be returned to be distributed in accordance with the court order.

If any part of a persons will appears to have no meaning or is ambiguous then the court will look at any surrounding evidence and the testators intention and will rectify the will in the light of this evidence.

The right to dispose of property

In general, the law allows an unfettered right to dispose of a persons property as they choose. This however is subject to tax and the courts powers to intervene. The law has been consolidated in the Inheritance (Provision for Family and Dependants Act) 1975. Certain categories of people can now apply to the court and be given money out of a deceased persons will. This can be done whether there is a will or not.

The husband or wife of a deceased person can be given any amount of money as the court thinks reasonable. The 1975 Act implemented the recommendations of the Law Commission which felt that a surviving spouse should be given money out of an estate on the same principles as a spouse is given money when there is a divorce. This means that, even if a will is not made, or there are inadequate provisions then a surviving spouse can make an application to rectify the situation.

The situation is different for other relations. They can apply to the court to have a will rectified but will receive far less than the spouse. The following can claim against a will:

- The wife or husband of the deceased
- A former wife or former husband of the deceased who has not remarried
- A child of the deceased
- Any person who is not included as a child of the deceased but who was treated by the deceased as a child of the family in relation to any marriage during his lifetime
- Any other person who was being maintained, even if only partly maintained, by the deceased just before his or her death

Former spouse

There is one main condition under which a former spouse can claim and that is that they have not remarried. In addition, such a claim would be for only essential maintenance which would stop on remarriage. There is one key exception, that is that if your death occurs within a year of divorce or legal separation, your former spouse can make a claim.

Child of the deceased

As the above, any claim by children can only be on the basis of hardship.

Stepchildren

This includes anyone treated as your own child and supported by you, including illegitimate children or those conceived before, but not born till after, your death. The claim can only cover essential maintenance.

Dependants

This covers a wide range of potential claimants. Maintenance only is payable. There needs to be evidence of full or partial maintenance prior to death. Such support does not have to be financial, however.

There is another situation where the court can change a will after your death. This relates directly to conditions that you may have imposed on a beneficiary in order to receive a gift which are unreasonable. If the court decides that this is the case, that particular condition becomes void and does not have to be fulfilled.

If the condition involved something being done before the beneficiary receives the gift then the beneficiary does not receive the gift. If the condition involved something being done after the beneficiary received the gift then the beneficiary can have the gift without condition. If the beneficiary does not receive the gift, as in the above, then either the will can make alternative provision or the gift can form part of the residue of the estate.

Unreasonable conditions can be many, one such being any condition that provides reason or incentive to break up a marriage, intention to remain celibate or not to remarry or one that separates children.

There are others which impinge on religion, general behaviour and crime. An unreasonable condition very much depends on the perception of the beneficiary and the perception of the courts.

A beneficiary can lose the right to a bequest, apart from any failure to meet conditions attached to a bequest. Again, a court will decide in what circumstance this is appropriate. Crime could be a reason, such as murder, or evidence of coercion or harassment of another person in pursuit of selfish gain.

9
Wills and Taxation

The formation of a will which enables you to minimise your tax liability is of the utmost importance. It is likely, if you are well off that you will want to consult a solicitor or financial advisor in order to gain the appropriate advice. It could be that you own a house which over the years has appreciated considerably which has resulted in the property being worth a considerable amount. This may mean that you could be liable for inheritance tax.

A book of this length cannot possibly give you in depth advice concerning your tax situation. However, what it can do is outline the current rules relating to tax and wills generally. It is very important to ensure that your will is updated regularly in order to keep abreast of the changing tax laws. The wealthier that you become the more important this becomes.

Deed of variation

Any change to a legal document is, in the main, achieved through a deed of variation. Within two years of a death, a beneficiary of a will may alter that deed in writing. For the purposes of inheritance tax the changed will is regarded as having been made by the dead person and substituted for that provision in the will or under the rules of intestacy. Tax will only be payable under the new provision. This is still true even if the beneficiary received the property and makes a gift of it or disclaims a legacy within two years of the death. The law governing this is set out in s. 142 Inheritance Tax Act 1984. In order to comply with s142 the disclaimer must be in writing, refer specifically to the provision in the will and be signed by the person making the change.

The deed should be sent as soon as possible to the Capital Taxes Office. Where a person redirects property or makes a gift of it within the two-year period he/she must give notice (written) to the Capital Taxes Office within six months of doing it that he wants this provision to apply. If the effect is to increase the liability to inheritance tax, then the executors must join in the notice and can refuse on the ground that they do not have sufficient assets in the estate to pay the extra tax.

Inheritance tax

Inheritance tax was introduced under the 1986 Finance Act to replace Capital Transfer Tax. It is a tax on what is known as "transfer of value" meaning transfer under the terms of a will, or the rules of intestacy which reduce an estate.

The amount which is liable to tax is the amount less any exemptions which are detailed further on. For tax purposes, the amount of the estate is the valuation of the estate of the dead person immediately before death. The tax is levied on transfers made by the dead person on death or *within seven years of death.*

Amount of inheritance tax payable

This is dependant on three factors:

- The value of the estate
- The value of any substantial gifts made within the last seven years
- Any exemptions from inheritance tax on ones death such as those on gifts to a surviving spouse, charities etc.

If a person is resident (domiciled) in the United Kingdom the tax applies to all that person property wherever it may be situated at home or abroad. If a person is domiciled abroad then the tax is applicable only to property in the United Kingdom.

The threshold for inheritance tax is 40% on the estate after exempt transfers and after the current tax threshold of £325,000 (2009/10) (check current provisions with your tax office). The amount is increased (usually) each year from 6th April in line with the increase in the Retail Price Index for the year to the previous December.

Exemptions from tax

The following are exempt for the purposes of inheritance tax liability:

- All gifts between the dead person and spouse. If the dead person is domiciled in the United Kingdom, and the husband/wife is not then the exemption is limited to £55,000.
- Lifetime gifts which represent normal expenditure out of the dead persons income during their life. Where payments are made by the dead person which did not change the dead persons standard of living then such amounts if paid seven years prior to the death will not be included in the estate.
- Lifetime gifts not exceeding £3000 in any one tax year. A person can make gifts totaling not more than £3000 in any year irrespective of the number of people to whom the amounts are given, otherwise any amounts over this will be included in the value of the estate if the person dies within seven years.
- Gifts in any one tax year to a maximum of £250 per person. There is no limit on the number of people to whom such gifts can be given so long as each one does not exceed £250 in any one tax year. These amounts are additional to the £3000

mentioned above but only to the extent that the total to any one individual in any tax year does not exceed £250.

- Gifts in consideration of marriage. Wedding gifts by a parent to his or her child are exempt by up to £5000, by a grandparent or other more distant relative up to £2500 and by other people up to £1000. This applies to each parent or grandparent.

- Lifetime gifts for the maintenance of a spouse or former spouse, children and dependant relatives. In respect of a child, the exemption is to the age of 18 or completion of full time education if later. This is available for stepchildren and adopted children, plus illegitimate children. The child must be of the donor or his or her spouse.

- All gifts to charities

- Gifts to political parties unless they are made within the year of the date of the death, in which case up to £100,000 is exempt, but any amount above that will be included in the value of the estate.

- Gifts to organisations which deal with preservation of the national heritage or of a public nature such as the British Museum. This category includes gifts to most museums and art galleries.

- Certain types of properties are exempt, including agricultural land, business property, historic houses and woodlands plus works of art.

Business property

Since 1992 there has been 100% relief for the following categories of business property:

- Sole proprietor or partner
- Life tenants business or interest in a business

- A holding of shares or securities which by itself, or in conjunction with other holdings owned by the transferor gives control of the company (whether quoted or unquoted)
- Unquoted shares which by themselves or in conjunction with other shares or securities owned by the transferor give control of more than 25% of the votes.

There is 50% relief for the following:

- Shares in a company which do not qualify under 3 above and which are not quoted on a recognised stock exchange.
- Land, buildings, plant or machinery owned by a partner or controlling shareholder and used wholly or mainly in the business of the partnership or company immediately before the transfer, provided that the partnership interest or shareholding would itself, if it were transferred, qualify for business relief.
- Any land or building, plant or machinery which, immediately before the transfer was used wholly for the purposes of a business carried on by the transferor, was settled property in which he or she was then beneficially entitled to an interest in possession and was transferred while the business itself was being retained.

Potentially Exempt Transfers

Any gift outside the exemptions mentioned above which is made within seven years of the persons death will be included in the value of the estate. Any gift made more than seven years from the death of the person making it is free of any liability for tax. These gifts are known as "Potentially Exempt Transfers" (PETS) and become wholly exempt once seven years have elapsed and the donor is still alive. If the donor dies within seven years of making the gift only a percentage of the tax payable will be due, depending on how long before the death it was made, in keeping with the following scale:

6-7 years   20% of gift at rate of 8%
5-6 years   40% of gift at rate of 16%
4-5 years   60% of gift at rate of 16%
3-4 years   80% of gift at rate of 32%
up to 3 years 100% of gift at rate of 40%

Life Insurance Policies

If a person has a life insurance policy on his or her life and for own benefit the value of the policy forms part of the estate. If there is a gift of the policy during that persons lifetime then the premium payment and not the policy becomes a potentially exempt transfer which will not be included in that persons estate if they survive seven years after the gift. If a policy is taken out for the benefit of another person it is the premium payment which is the PET and not the value of the policy.

Policies such as this can be a useful way of making provision for inheritance tax liability on an estate as a whole.

Gifts with reservation

One way in which a person may seek to minimise inheritance tax liability is to reduce the value of the estate by making gifts before death. As demonstrated, these will be regarded as PETS and may be brought into the estate if death occurs within seven years. There is another factor to be considered. If a person gives something away but still continues to enjoy it or derive a benefit from it, then such a gift will form part of the estate whenever it was made so long as the donor continued to enjoy it up to his or her death. This is known as a "gift with reservation" because the donor reserves a benefit. To avoid a gift with reservation, the gift must be enjoyed by the person to whom it has been given.

The payment of tax

Whenever money is left in a will consideration needs to be given as to whether inheritance tax attributable to it is to be paid out of the residue of the estate or to be paid by the person receiving the legacy. If inheritance tax comes from the residue of the estate then it should be declared to be free of tax, if paid by the person to whom it is left, it is declared subject to tax.

Deductions from the estate

From the overall value of the estate for inheritance tax purposes, reasonable funeral expenses can be deducted. In addition, any additional expenses incurred in administering or realising property outside of the United Kingdom against its value (to a maximum of 50%) can be realised.

Gifts to charitable institutions

Gifts to charities are exempt at any time whether as lifetime gifts or passed under the terms of a will. They can be expressed as either to a specific charity or as an amount to be distributed by the dead persons trustees. These can be the same as the executors in which case they should be named as trustees as well as executors.

In many cases a person will make a will many years before death. This could mean that unless a will is revised regularly, the amounts of money specified as bequests may become devalued through inflation so that on death they no longer represent the original size of the gift that was intended.

One common way of overcoming this is to express the gift as a percentage or proportion of the overall net estate.

If you wish a bequest to go to a specific branch of a charity this must be specified, otherwise the gift will go to head office as a matter of course.

10

Making a Will in Scotland

There are a number of key differences for a will made in Scotland, which need to be highlighted:

- Intestacy

If you do not make a will in Scotland before you die, the law is a s follows:

- If there is a spouse but no other close family, such as children, parents, brothers and sisters etc, then the spouse benefits from the whole estate.
- If there is a spouse and there are children, then the spouse can have property (or £50,000 if it is worth more) furniture and personal possessions up to a value of £10,000, cash up to £15,000 and a third of the remainder of the state (excluding other property). Children (or their children) share what is left in equal proportion.
- If there is no spouse but there are children then they or their children benefit from the estate in equal shares. (not stepchildren).
- If there is no spouse or children, but there are parents, brothers and sisters then the parents take half of the estate and the other half is divided equally between any brothers and sisters or their

children. Where only one of these groups is alive, those concerned benefit from the whole estate.

If none of the above applies, then the following benefit, in this order:

- Full uncles/aunts or their children
- Half uncles/aunts or their children
- Grandparents
- Full great uncles/aunts (or descendants)
- Half great uncles/aunts (or descendants)
- Great grandparents

If no relatives can be found then the Crown takes the estate and can distribute it among anyone with a reasonable claim.

- **Age**

Whereas in the rest of the United Kingdom you need to be over 18 to make a will, in Scotland the age limit is lower. For a male it is over fourteen and twelve for a female.

- **Marriage**

In Scotland, marriage does not revoke a will.

- **Children**

Elsewhere in the United Kingdom this applies to illegitimate and adopted children, in Scotland you have to specify their status in the will. If you have children after making a will and have not made any mention of them the will is considered null and void. A new will needs to be produced.

- **Presentation**

If you produce the whole of your will by hand, then you do not need any witnesses. You must sign at the bottom of every page, not just the last page. If the will is not completely handwritten then you will need two witnesses.

- **Claims against your estate**

In Scotland, the spouse and children have more rights to claim against the estate than the rest of the United Kingdom, even if there is provision in the will to specifically exclude them. The law equally applies against any claims from others who were partly or totally dependent on the dead person before death.

11

The Serviceman's Will

The minimum age limit applicable generally does not apply in the case of servicemen on active military service. These laws only apply in operational conditions-that is in a war situation.

The will itself can either be in writing or can be passed on orally to a witness. The witness can be a beneficiary and can receive gifts from the estate.

In the case of a written will this can be in handwriting and does not have to be witnessed. If the person gives verbal instructions as to how he or she wants the estate to be disposed of, all that is required is a clear intention that such instructions should be carried out if and indeed when the situation requires it.

A will can be revoked by similar means, that is by hand or mouth. This is only applicable if that person remains in the armed forces.

Where a person dies on active service, there is no inheritance tax on the estate.

PART 2

OBTAINING PROBATE AND ADMINISTERING ESTATES

12

Administering Estates

The formalities

Relatives or friends of the deceased will take on the task of dealing with the necessary formalities after death. In the first instance, notwithstanding where the person dies, a doctor must provide relatives with a certificate stating the cause of death. This certificate is then lodged at the Registry of Births Deaths and marriages within five days of the issue. The registrar will need to know full details of the death and will also ask for any other certificates such as marriage and birth. The person who registers the death is known as the 'informant'.

If the doctor states that the cause of death is uncertain, then the arrangements are rather more complex. The death will first be reported to the coroner, who usually orders a post-mortem. If it shows that the cause of death was natural, the coroner then authorises the burial or cremation. In these cases, you will be issued with a death certificate by the Registrar and a second certificate permitting the undertaker to arrange burial or cremation.

Except in rare cases, for example violent death when the coroner orders an inquest to be held, it will now be time to organise the funeral. It will be necessary at this point to check the will or if there is no will, to find out about the arrangements for administering the estate.

Funeral arrangements

If there is a will in existence, it may well contain details concerning the desired funeral arrangements of the deceased. If there are no clear instructions the executors of the will usually make appropriate arrangements. The executor will become legally liable to pay costs of the funeral.

Where the deceased dies intestate, the 'administrators' of the estate will instruct the undertaker and assume responsibility for payments. In some cases, it may be clear that the deceased does not have enough assets to cover the funeral. If this is the case then investigations need to take place, including the possibility of a one-off funeral grant to cover costs. Once financial details have been settled it is advisable to put a notice in the deaths column of one or more papers to bring the funeral to the attention of relatives.

The responsibilities of executors

Executors and administrators of estates have very important responsibilities. In the first instance they are responsible for ensuring that the assets of the estate are paid to the correct beneficiaries of the will and also for ensuring that all debts are paid before distribution. If this aspect of administration is mismanaged then the executor or administrator will be held, or could be held, liable for any debts. In order to ensure that they are protected then executors or administrators should advertise in the London gazette – which is a newspaper for formal notices of any kind, and also a local paper together with requests that creditors should submit their claims by a date which must be at least two months after the advertisement. Private individuals will usually have to produce a copy of probate before their advertisement is accepted for publication.

The executor's initial steps

If you are the executor of a valid will (or if you are the administrator if there is no will) you can now begin the task of administering the estate.

It will be essential to ensure that the basic elements are dealt with such as informing utilities, arranging for termination of certain insurance policies and discharge of liabilities of others such as life insurance. Arrangements will need to be made for any pets and post redirected. These are the basic essential lifestyle elements before you make an application for probate.

The value of the estate

Before you can apply for probate of the will, you have to find out the extent and value of the assets and liabilities of the estate. You will need to have access to all records of assets, such as insurance policies and bank accounts. The ease with which you can establish a total value will depend on how organised the deceased was. If the deceased was a taxpayer it is advisable to approach the local tax office for a copy of his or her last tax return, sending a copy of the will to prove your status as an executor.

Once you have collated all proof of assets including property you will need to arrive at a total value. The following will provide a pointer for establishing value:

Bank accounts
Interest-bearing accounts and joint bank accounts

When you have found out details of these accounts you should ask for details of balance and accrued interest at the time of death. This is needed for the tax return you will have to complete on behalf of the deceased estate.

These types of accounts can be problematic. If the joint holders are husband and wife, the account will pass automatically to the survivor. In other cases you will need to establish the intentions of the joint owners or the contribution of each to the joint account. This is because the amount contributed by the deceased forms part of the estate for tax purposes (except where a written agreement confirms that the money in the account passes automatically to the survivor). In the case of business partnership accounts, you need a set of final trading accounts to the date of death and should contact the surviving partner.

National Savings

These may take the form of National Savings Certificates, National Savings Investment Accounts or Premium Bonds. A claim form for repayment should be obtained, usually from the post office and sent to the appropriate department for National Savings together with a copy of the probate when you have it.

Building societies

You would approach a building society in the same way as a bank, asking for a balance and interest to date. You should also ask for a claim form for payment.

Life insurance

You should write to insurance companies stating the date of death and the policy number and enclose a copy of the death certificate. Once probate has been obtained submit your claim form for monies owed. In many cases, policies are held on trust and will not form part of an estate. Insurance companies will, on production of the death certificate, make payment direct to the beneficiaries.

Stock and shares

You should make arrangements to forward a list of stocks and shares held by the deceased to a bank or stockbroker. In the case of Pep's and

ISA's you should send them to the plan manger and ask for a valuation. Ask for transfer forms for all shareholdings.

You may decide to value the stocks and shares yourself. If this is the case, you will need a copy of the official Stock Exchange Daily Official List for the day on which the deceased died. The valuation figure is calculated by adding 25% of the difference between the selling and buying prices. If the death took place at the weekend you can choose either the Monday or Friday Valuation. However, if the executors sell any shares at a loss within 12 months, the selling price in all cases can be taken as the value at the date of death.

If you cannot locate all of the share certificates, you may be able to find dividend counterfoils or tax vouchers among the papers of the deceased which will enable you to check the number of shares held in the company. If you cannot find share certificates, write to the Registrar of the company. Name of Registrars are given in the Register of Registrars held in the local library. The same approach can be made if the deceased holds unit trusts. In the case of private companies where no value of shares is published, you may sometimes be able to obtain a valuation from the secretary of the company. In the case of a family company it will usually be necessary to have the value determined by a private accountant.

Pensions

If the deceased was already receiving a pension, you should write to the company operating the scheme in order to find out further details, i.e. is the pension paid up until the time of death, are there any other beneficiaries after death and so on. Pensions vary significantly and it is very important that accurate information is obtained.

State benefits

If the deceased was in receipt of an old age pension, notice of the death should be given to the Department of Work and Pensions, so that any adjustments can be made. In the case of married men, the agency will make arrangements to begin to pay widows pension.

Businesses

The valuation of a business on the death of one of the partners is complicated and depends upon the nature of the business, the way in which the accounts are prepared and the extent of the assets held by the business. The surviving partner/s should make available a set of partnership accounts to the date of death and help you to determine the correct valuation for the deceased share.

Farms

If the deceased had an interest in a farm, any type of farm you should seek advice of a more specialist agricultural valuer.

Residential property

If the estate is below the inheritance tax threshold, you may be able to estimate the value of the property by looking at similar properties in estate agents windows. You may also wish to obtain a professional valuation. If the estate reaches the inheritance tax threshold or is close to it, the figure is checked by the District Valuer. If the property is sold within four years of death for less than the probate valuation, and providing the sellers are executors and not beneficiaries, the sale price may be substituted for the original valuation.

In the case of joint properties, the value of the person who has died forms part of the estate for tax purposes. However, if the share passes to the spouse, the 'surviving spouse exemption' applies. This means that there is no inheritance tax to pay, even if the estate exceeds the inheritance tax threshold.

If there is a mortgage on the property at the date of death, the amount of the debt must be found by writing to the bank or building society. The value of the house is reduced by this amount.

Where the deceased has left residential property as a specific item, the will may either say that the property is to be transferred to the beneficiary free from any mortgage or that it is subject to a mortgage, The Administration of Estates Act provides that a person who is bequeathed a mortgaged property is responsible repaying the mortgage unless the will sets out a contrary intention.

Other property and buildings
If the deceased owned commercial property, the executor has to determine whether this was a business asset or whether it is an investment property unconnected with any business. If this is the case a separate valuation will be needed.

Personal possessions
Although it is not always necessary to obtain professional valuations for household goods, estimated values are examined very carefully by the District Valuer if the estate is large enough to attract inheritance tax. The way household goods are dealt with will depend entirely on their value. In certain cases, with items such as painting and jewellery then an auction may be appropriate.

Income tax
It is very unlikely that, before you make your application for probate, you will be in a position to calculate the income tax owed on an estate. As the administration of the estate gathers momentum then you will

amass enough information to start forming a picture of the value and thus the tax liabilities.

13

Applying For Probate

Applying for Probate

Probate represents the official proof the validity of a will and is granted by the court on production by the executors of the estate of the necessary documents. Only when probate is obtained are executors free to administer and distribute the estate.

If the value of the estate is under £5000 in total, it may be possible to administer the estate without obtaining probate. Generally, if the estate is worth more than £5000, you will have to apply for probate of the will or letters of administration. There are a number of reasons for this:

- Banks, building societies and National Savings are governed by the Administration of Estates (Small payments) Act 1965. This only allows them to refund individual accounts up to £5000 without production of probate.

- You cannot sell stocks, shares or land from an estate without probate, except in the case of land held in names of joint tenants where this passes on after death

- If the administration is disputed or if a person intends to make a claim as a dependant or member of the family, his or her claim is 'statute barred' six months after the grant of probate. The right to take action remains open if the estate is administered without probate

- A lay executor who managed to call in the assets of an estate without probate might miss the obligation to report matters to the Inland Revenue for inheritance tax purposes, especially where a substantial gift had been made in the seven years prior to the death.

Letters of administration

If someone dies intestate (without making a will) the rules of intestacy laid down by Act of Parliament will apply. An administrator must apply for letters of administration for exactly the same reasons as the executor applies for probate. The grant of letters of administration will be made to the first applicant.

If a will deals with part only but not all of the administration (for example where the will defines who receives what but does not name an executor) the person entitled to apply for letters of administration make the application to the Registrar attaching the will at the same time. The applicant is granted 'Letters of administration with will attached'.

Applying for letters of administration

The following demonstrates the order of those entitled to apply:
- The surviving spouse (not unmarried partner)
- The children or their descendants (once over 18)
- If there are no children or descendants of those children who are able to apply, the parents of the deceased can apply
- Brothers and sisters 'of the half blood'
- Grandparents
- Aunts and uncles of the whole blood
- Aunts and uncles of the half blood
- The Crown (or Duchy of Lancaster or Duchy of Cornwall) if there are no blood relations.

Where the estate is insolvent other creditors have the right to apply.

The probate registry – applying for probate

The first step is to obtain the necessary forms from the personal application department of the Principal Probate Registry in London or the local district probate registry. The more straightforward cases can usually be handled by post or by one visit to the probate registry. The executor will complete and send in the forms, they are checked and the amount of probate fees and inheritance tax assessed. The registry officials prepare the official document which the executor then swears, attending personally to do so. The process from submission to swearing usually takes three to four weeks.

Filling in the forms

The necessary forms for applying for probate can be obtained from the probate registry. These are:

- Form PA1 – the probate application form
- Form 1HT 205 – the return of assets and debts

With the forms you will receive other items which serve as guidance to the forms and process:

- 1HT 206 – notes to help you with 1HT 205
- Form PA1 (A) – guidance notes for completing PA1
- Form PA3 – a list of local probate offices
- Form PA4 – a table of fees payable

Form PA1 is fairly uncomplicated. The form is split into white and blue sections with the applicant filling in the white sections. The form will ask which office the applicant wants to attend, details of the deceased, the will and something about you. In cases where more than one executor is involved, the registrar will usually correspond with one executor only. The form also has a space for naming any executors who cannot apply for probate, e.g. because they do not want to or have died since the will was written. If they may apply at a later date, the probate office will send an official 'power reserved letter' which the non-acting executor signs. This is a useful safeguard in case the first executor dies or becomes incapacitated before grant of probate is obtained.

You do not have to sign form PA1. At the end of the process, the probate registry will couch the information you supply in legal jargon for the document you are required to sign.

Form PA1 contains a reminder that you have to attach the death certificate, the will and the completed form 1HT 205. If this form demonstrates that the estate exceeds the 'excepted estate' threshold (for inheritance tax purposes) form 1HT 200 will have to be completed.

Sending the forms

If the estate you are administering can be contained on form 1HT 205, you are ready to send in your application. Make sure that you take photocopies of all material. You should send the following:

- The will
- The death certificate
- Probate application form PA1
- Short form 1HT 205
- A cheque for the fee

Attach any explanatory letter as necessary. You should then send the package by registered post. A few weeks later, you will be invited to review the documents, pay the probate fee and swear the prescribed oath. Remember to take your file of background papers.

Probate fees are calculated on the amount of the net estate, as declared for the purpose of inheritance tax. Fees are payable when you attend the interview at the registry – see form PA4 for guidance.

Attendance at the probate registry

When you arrive at the probate registry you will need to examine the forms that have been prepared for you. You need to satisfy yourself that all the details are correct. When you have checked all the details, the commissioner will ask you to sign the original will and swear the oath, identifying the will as that of the deceased.

The actual process entails you standing up, holding a copy of the New Testament and repeating the words spoken by the commissioner. The words take the form of 'I swear by Almighty God that this is my name and handwriting and that the contents of this my oath are true and that this is the will referred to'. The form of oath is varied depending on religious belief or otherwise.

The commissioner will then sign beneath your signature on the official form and will. The fees are paid and any sealed copies as ordered will be supplied.

Letters of administration

If the deceased has left no will, then the next of kin will apply for a grant of letters of administration instead of probate. The same is the case if a will was left but no executors appointed. In these cases, the grant is called 'letters of administration with will annexed'

When letters of administration are sought, the administrators may in some cases have to provide a guarantee – for example where the beneficiaries are under age or mentally disabled or when the administrator is out of the country. The guarantee is provided by an insurance company at a cost or by individuals who undertake to make good – up to the gross value of the estate – any deficiency caused by the administrators failing in their duties.

Letters of administration may also be taken out by creditors of an estate if executors deliberately do not apply for probate – for instance, if the estate has insufficient assets to pay all creditors and legatees.

Inheritance tax and form 1HT 200

Form 1HT 200 is the Inland Revenue account for inheritance tax. It should be completed by reference to form 1HT 210, guidance notes. 1HT consists of eight pages. Take time and care with this form. It is relatively uncomplicated. Please refer to the appendix for an example.

The grant of probate

There may be a time lapse of six weeks or more between lodging the probate papers and the meeting at the registry to sign and swear them. After this has happened, however, things move quickly. If there is no inheritance tax to be paid – where the net estate is less than £240,000, or where the deceased property goes to the spouse – the grant of probate (or letters of administration) is issued within a few days. If inheritance tax is due, it takes two to three weeks before the exact amount is calculated and the grant is usually ready about a week later.

The grant of probate is signed by an officer of the probate registry. Attached to the grant of probate is a photocopy of the will. (all original wills are kept at the Principal Probate Registry in London). Each page of your copy of the will carries the impress of the courts official seal. It is accompanied by a note which explains the procedure for collecting and distributing the estate and advises representatives to take legal advice in the event of dispute or other difficulty.

14

The Distribution of The Estate

The distribution of the estate of the deceased

Having established probate, it is now time to begin to distribute the estate. Before you can do this, however, it is essential that you understand exactly what the will says. The executor can be sued for payment if the estate is not distributed exactly in accordance with the stipulations in the will. Although this may sound like common sense, some wills may be couched in a particular way, or in a particular jargon and you may need advice on the interpretation.

Specific legacies and bequests

Legacies are, usually, the payment of specific sums of money. Bequests usually mean gifts of goods or cash. 'Devises' means gifts of land or buildings. If the state is not subject to inheritance tax and the legacies and bequests are small, legacies can be paid without further delay and also specific items can be handed over. It is advisable to obtain a receipt from the beneficiary(s) when they receive their gift or legacy. One common problem that can arise is trying to trace beneficiaries. This is usually done through the local or national press if the beneficiary is not forthcoming.

Transferring property

If a beneficiary has been left a house or other property then any outstanding debts relating to the property, such as a mortgage have to be dealt with. The will usually directs the executors to pay off the mortgage. However, if the will is silent on this point then it will become the responsibility of the beneficiary. It is quite usual that a property is left to another with a mortgage and equity in the property so the beneficiary can continue to pay.

It will be necessary to transfer the property into your own name by contacting the Land Registry. If the property is already registered, as is most property, the process will be straightforward. However, if it is unregistered then you will need to obtain a first registration. You would probably need to instruct a solicitor to do this. At the same time obtain advice about settling the mortgage.

Preparation of final accounts

Having gathered the assets and obtained a good idea of the value you can now begin to prepare final accounts. There is no set form for the final accounts but assets and liabilities must be included, receipts and payments made during the administration and a distribution account of payments to beneficiaries.

It is helpful to include a covering sheet to the accounts, a form of memorandum which will cover the following areas:

- Details of the deceased and date of death, date of probate and names of executors
- A summary of the bequests made in the will
- Particulars of property transfers
- Reference to any valuations which have been included in the accounts

In estates where inheritance tax has been paid, you should prepare one part of the capital account based on the value of the assets at the time of death.

The second part of the account should demonstrate the value of those assets and liabilities at the date they are realised or paid. If the net effect is to reduce the value of the estate, you may be able to claim a refund from the capital taxes office. Conversely you may have increased taxes to pay. In either case you should advise the capital taxes office.

A model set of accounts are shown in the appendix. The capital account shows the value of assets when they are cashed or realised and the debts are the sums actually paid. The income account shows the income received during the administration, less associated expenses. It is convenient to run this account from the date of death to the following 5th of April.

The distribution account shows the capital and income transferred from the respective accounts and how the residue of the estate has been divided. If there is only one beneficiary you should show the final figure. If any items have been taken in kind – such as a car or a piece of furniture – its value is included in the distribution account as both an asset and payment. If you are claiming executor's expenses itemise them and include them in the distribution account.

Where a will exists

When you have completed your accounts, and all outstanding debts and liabilities have been met, you will now be in a position to calculate how much each residuary beneficiary receives according to the specific provisions of the will. In practice, the amount that you have left in the executor's bank account should match the sums to be paid out.

After having ascertained that this is the case, and rectified any errors you should send the accounts to the beneficiaries for their agreement or otherwise. In cases involving inheritance tax, you should contact the capital taxes office and confirm that you have disclosed the full value of the estate. You then apply for a clearance certificate. When you have received this you can make the final distribution to the beneficiaries.

The beneficiaries should be asked to sign an acknowledgement that they agree the accounts and that they agree the amount that they will receive.

Where beneficiaries are deceased or missing

If a beneficiary dies before the death of the testator, the general rule is that the legacy cannot be made. There are a few exceptions to this rule:

- If the will contains a 'substitution' (an alternative to the beneficiary)
- If the gift is made to two people as joint tenants – the survivor being the beneficiary
- If section 33(2) of the Wills Act 1837 applies. This section provides that, if the share of the estate or gift is to a child or other descendant of the testator and the child dies before the testator leaving 'issue' (children and their descendants) they take the share of the gift.

If a beneficiary cannot be located, you must take steps to find that person. These steps must be reasonable. As stated, an advertisement can suffice, as well as contacting relatives and so on. You can apply to the court for an order giving you permission to distribute the estate on agreed terms You can claim any expenses incurred from the estate.

It is very important, if you cannot find a beneficiary that you take steps to obtain a court order in order to protect yourself from any future problems arising should a beneficiary turn up.

The children's trust under intestacy rules

We saw earlier in the book how an estate is distributed according to the rules of intestacy. When the surviving spouse has children, whatever their age, and the estate is worth more than £125,000, the administrators of the estate must set up a trust to look after the children's share. As trustees, they must invest half the remaining capital in their own names. They notify the Inland Revenue of the new trust and submit a Trust Tax return each year. The income from the trust is paid to the spouse. On the death of the spouse, the capital held in the trust account is shared between the children unless they are under 18.

If any of the children die, leaving children of their own, before the death of the intestate or – whichever is the later – second parent, the Statutory Trust rules apply. Under these rules, where a child of the intestate has died leaving children who are 18 or over (or who marry before 18) the children get their parents share. The same applies if the only survivors are grandchildren or even remote descendants.

In some cases, intestacy rules can be rigid and cause hardship. You should always take advice when dealing with distribution of assets in cases that are complicated to resolve.

Glossary of terms

Administrator
The person who administers the estate of a person who has died intestate

Bequest
A gift of a particular object or cash as opposed to 'devise' which means land or buildings

Chattels
Personal belongings of the deceased

Child
Referred to in a will or intestacy – child of the deceased including adopted and illegitimate children but, unless specifically included in a will, not stepchildren

Cohabitee
A partner of the deceased who may be able to claim a share of the estate. The term 'common law wife' has no legal force.

Confirmation
The document issued to executors by the sheriff court in Scotland to authorise them to administer the estate

Devise
A gift of house or land

Disposition
A formal conveyancing document in Scotland

Estate
Al the assets and property of the deceased, including houses, cars, investments, money and personal belongings

Executor
The person appointed in the will to administer the estate of a deceased person

Heritable estate
Land and buildings in Scotland

Inheritance tax
The tax which may be payable when the total estate of the deceased person exceeds a set threshold (subject to various exemptions and adjustments)

Intestate
A person who dies without making a will

Issue
Al the descendants of a person, i.e. children, grandchildren, great grandchildren#

Legacy
A gift of money

Minor
A person under 18 years of age

Moveable estate
Property other than land or buildings in Scotland

Next of Kin
The person entitled to the estate when a person dies intestate

Letters of administration
The document issued to administrators by a probate registry to authorise them to administer the estate of an intestate

Personal estate or personalty
Al the investments and belongings of a person apart from land and buildings

Personal representatives
A general term for both administrators and executors

Probate of the will
The document issued to executors by a probate registry in England, Wales and Northern Ireland to authorise them to administer the estate

Probate Registry
The Government office which deals with probate maters. The principal Probate Registry is in London with district registries in cities and some large towns

Real estate or realty
Land and buildings owned by a person

Residue

What is left of the estate to share out after all the debts and specific bequests and legacies have been paid

Specific bequests

Particular items gifted by will

Testator

A person who makes a will

Will

The document in which you say what is to happen to your estate after death

Useful Addresses

Department for National Savings
Glasgow G58 1SB
For enquiries about Capital Bonds, Childrens Bonus Bonds, FIRST Option Bonds, Fixed Rate Savings Bonds, Ordinary Accounts and Investment Accounts.

Department for National Savings
Durham DH99 1NS
Enquiries about deposit bonds, Cash mini-ISA's Savings Certificates, SAYE Contracts and Yearly Plan Agreements

Department for National Savings
Blackpool FY3 9YP
Enquiries about Premium Bonds, Pensioners guaranteed bonds

Tel 0845 964 5000 (Central Helpline)
www.nationalsavings.co.uk

Department of Work and Pensions
Newcastle Benefits Directorate
Cathedral Square
Newcastle Upon Tyne NE1 1EE

For pensions enquiries
0191 152000
www.dss.gov.uk

HM Revenue and Customs Capital Taxes Office
Ferrers House
PO Box 38
Castle Meadow Road
Nottingham NG2 1BB
0115 742400
www.inlandrevenue.gov.org

The Law Society of England and Wales
113 Chancery lane
London WC2A 1PL
0207 242 1222
Public information including solicitors who specialise in wills and probate
www.lawsociety.org.uk

London Gazette
PO Box 7923
London SE1 5ZH
020 7394 4517

Office for the Supervision of Solicitors
Victoria Court
8 Dormer Place
Leamington Spa
Warwickshire CV32 5AE
01926 820082

www.solicitors-online.com
Information on solicitors specialising in wills and probate

The Principal Probate Registry
First Avenue House
42-49 High Holborn
London WC1V 6NP
0845 3020 900
www.courtservice.gov.uk

OYEZ Straker
PO Box 55
7 Spa road
London SE16 3QQ
0207 556 3345

Useful Addresses in Scotland
Accountant of Court
2 Parliament Square
Edinburgh EH1 1RQ
0131 240 6742
www.scotscourts.gov.uk

HMRC Capital Taxes
Meldrum House
15 Drumsheugh Gardens
Edinburgh EH3 7UG
0131 777 4343 (helpline)
www.inlandrevenue.gov.uk (home pages download leaflets free of charge)
www.inlandrevenue.gov.cto.iht.htm (Inheritance tax)

Law Society of Scotland
26 Drumsheugh Gardens
Edinburgh EH3 7YR
0131 226 7411 (Head Office) www.lawscot.org.uk

Registers of Scotland
Customer Service Centre
Erskine House
68 Queen Street
Edinburgh EH2 4NF
0845 607 0161
Or
Registers of Scotland
Customer Service Centre
9 George Square
Glasgow G2 1DY
Tel 0845 6070164
www.ros.gov.uk

Sheriff Clerks Office
Commissary Department
27 Chambers Street
Edinburgh EH1 1LB
0131 225 2525

Appendix 1 Example of Administration Accounts

In the Estate of   Deceased.
Date of death

CAPITAL ACCOUNT
Assets

House Net sales proceeds	£145,000
(value at death £155,000)	
Less mortgage	£95,000
	£50,000
Stocks and shares	£89,000
(value at death £86500)	
Life policy	£7500
Skipton BS deposit	£9000
Interest to date of death	£75
National Savings – Premium bonds	£7000
Arrears of pension	£325
Agreed value of house contents	£3800
Car	£5600
Gross estate	£172,300
Less debts and liabilities	
Funeral costs	£2000

Gas	£270
Electricity	£25
Administration expenses	£45
Probate fees	£130
Stockbrokers valuation fee	£250
Income tax paid to date of death	£650

Inheritance tax paid on application for probate (N/a) estate less than £240,000

Net Estate carried to distribution account

£168930

For the estate to attract inheritance tax the value would need to be above £240,000. If that is the case, carry on the calculation for inheritance tax by multiplying the residue after £240,000 by 40% which will give you the inheritance tax due.

In the estate of   Deceased

Income account
Dividends received for period from 1st October 2008 to 5th April 2009

Holding	Company	Net dividend
5000 shares	ABC PLC	£1400
4300 shares	Halifax PLC	£560
12000 shares	GKN	£1420
3760 shares	Powergen	£420
Savings accounts final interest		£150

Balance transferred to distribution account

£3950

In the estate of   Deceased

Distribution account
Balance transferred from capital account   £168930
Balance transferred from income account   £3950

£172880

Less payment of legacies

David Peters   £5000

Net residuary estate for distribution   £167880

Mr Frederick Dillon

A one half share represented by

  a)   House contents   £3800
  b)   The balance   £80140

Stella Donaldson
One half share represented by the balance   £83940
Total

£167880

Appendix 2 – Example forms to be used in the process of probate

1. N205D-NOTICE OF ISSUE (PROBATE CLAIM)
2. PA1-HOW TO OBTAIN PROBATE
3. GUIDANCE NOTES FOR FORM PA1
4. APPLICATION FOR A PROBATE SEARCH
5. PA2-HOW TO OBTAIN PROBATE-GUIDE FOR THE APPLICANT WITHOUT SOLICITOR.
6. PROBATE FEES PA3
7. PROBATE REGISTRIES AND LOCAL INTERVIEW VENUES
8. MY PROBATE APPOINTMENT-WHAT HAPPENS NEXT?

Notice of issue
(probate claim)

In the

Claim No.

Claimant(s)

Defendant(s)

Issue fee

In the estate of

deceased (Probate)

Your claim was issued on [   ]

[The court sent it to the defendant(s) by first class post on [   ]

and it will be deemed served on [   ]].

[The claim form (which includes particulars of claim) is returned to you, with the relevant response forms, for

you to serve them on the defendant(s)]

Notes for guidance
The claim form and particulars of claim, if served separately, must be served on the defendant within 4 months
of the date of issue (6 months if you are serving outside England and Wales). You may be able to apply to
extend the time for serving the claim form but the application must generally be made before the 4 month or
6 month period expires.

You must inform the court immediately if your claim is settled.

The defendant must file an acknowledgment of service and defence within 28 days of service of the Particulars
of Claim (whether they are served with the claim form or separately). A longer period applies if the defendant
is served outside England and Wales.

Default judgment **cannot** be obtained in a probate claim.

If no defendant acknowledges service or files a defence, and the time for doing so has expired, you may apply to
the court for an order that the claim proceed to trial.

To

Ref.

Probate Application Form - PA1

Please use **BLOCK CAPITALS**

Name of deceased	
Interview venue	
Dates to avoid	

Please read the following questions and PA2 booklet 'How to obtain probate' carefully before filling in this form. Please also refer to the Guidance Notes enclosed where an item is marked *.

PLEASE COMPLETE ALL SECTIONS.

		This column is for official use
	Section A: The Will / Codicil	

A1 Did the deceased leave a will/codicil? *(Note: These may not necessarily be formal documents. If the answer to question 1 is Yes, you must enclose the **original** document(s) with your application.)*

Will Yes ☐ No ☐   **Codicil** Yes ☐ No ☐

Date of will

Date of codicil

If **No** to both questions, please go to Section B

A2 Did the deceased marry or enter into a Civil Partnership after the date of the will/codicil?   Yes ☐ Date: No ☐

A3 Is there anyone under 18 years old who receives anything in the will/codicil?   Yes ☐ No ☐

A4 Did any of the witnesses to the will or codicil or the spouse/civil partner of any witness receive a gift under the will/codicil? If Yes, state name of witness.   Yes ☐ No ☐

A5 Are there any executors named in the will/codicil?   Yes ☐ No ☐

A6 Give the names of those executors who are **not** applying and the reasons why. **Note:** All executors **must** be accounted for.

Full names	Reason A,B,C,D,E

A = Pre-deceased
B = Died after the deceased
C = Power Reserved
D = Renunciation
E = Power of Attorney

B1 - B6

Please refer to the Guidance Notes.

Sections B1 - B4 must be completed in all cases.

Please state the **number** of relatives of the deceased in categories B1 - B4.

If there are no relatives in a particular category, write 'nil' in each box and move onto the next category.

Note: Sections B5 and B6 only need to be completed if the deceased had no relatives in Section B1 - B4.

Section B: Relatives of the deceased

Number of relatives (if none, write nil)	Under 18	Over 18
B1 Surviving **lawful** husband or wife or surviving **lawful** civil partner		
B2a Sons or daughters who survived the deceased		
b Sons or daughters who did **not** survive the deceased		
c Children of person(s) indicated at '2b' **only**, who survived the deceased *		
B3 Parents who survived the deceased		
B4a Brothers or sisters who survived the deceased		
b Brothers or sisters who did **not** survive the deceased		
c Children of person(s) indicated at '4b' **only**, who survived the deceased *		
B5 Grandparents who survived the deceased		
B6a Uncles or aunts who survived the deceased		
b Uncles or aunts who did **not** survive the deceased		
c Children of person(s) indicated at '6b' **only**, who survived the deceased *		

Please note that the grant will normally be sent to the first applicant. Any applicant named will be required to attend an interview. It is, however, usually only necessary for one person to apply (please see PA2 booklet, page 3).

Section C: Details of applicant(s)

This column is for official use

C1	Title	Mr ☐ Mrs ☐ Miss ☐ Ms ☐ Other [ ]
C2	Forenames	
C3	Surname	
C4	Address	

I.T.W.C

Postcode:

C5	Telephone number	Home
		Work
	E-mail address (optional)	
C6	Occupation	

C7 Are you related to the deceased?　　Yes ☐　　No ☐

If Yes, what is your relationship?　　Relationship:

C8 If there are any other applicants, up to a maximum of three, give their details. (Note: **All** applicants named in Sections C1 and C8 must attend an interview.)

Details of other applicants who wish to be named in the grant of representation. (Please give details as C1 to C7 including relationship to deceased.)

C9 Name and address of any surviving lawful husband or wife/civil partner of the deceased, unless stated above.

Postcode:

*C10 If you are applying as an attorney on behalf of the person entitled to the grant, please state their name, address and capacity in which they are entitled (e.g. relationship to the deceased).

Postcode:

Relationship:

*C10a Have you been appointed by the person entitled as their attorney under an Enduring Power of Attorney (EPA) or a Property and financial affairs Lasting Power of Attorney (LPA)?

EPA ☐　　LPA ☐　　No ☐

*C10b If Yes, has it been registered with the Office of the Public Guardian?

Yes ☐　　No ☐

*C10c Does the donor of the EPA/LPA lack mental capacity within the meaning of the Mental Capacity Act 2005? *(see PA1a)*

Yes ☐　　No ☐

	Section D: Details of the deceased	This column is for official use
*D1 Forenames		
*D2 Surname		True name
*D3 Did the deceased hold any assets **(excluding joint assets)** in another name?	Yes ☐ No ☐	Alias
*D4a If Yes, what are the assets?		
And in what name(s) are they held?		Address
D4b Was the deceased known by any other name in which he/she made a will? If so, what name was it made in?	Yes ☐ No ☐	
D5 Last permanent address of the deceased.		
		D/C district and No.
	Postcode:	
D6 Date of birth		
D7 Date of death	Age:	L.S.A.
Domicile ***D8** Was England and Wales the domicile/permanent home of the deceased at the date of death? If No, please specify the deceased's permanent home or domicile.	Yes ☐ No ☐	D.B.F.
*D9 Tick the last **legal** marital or civil partnership status of the deceased, and give dates where appropriate.	Bachelor/Spinster ☐ Widow/Widower/Surviving Civil Partner ☐ Married/Civil Partnership ☐ Date: Divorced/Civil Partnership dissolved ☐ Date: Judicially separated ☐ Date:	
Note: These documents (✦) may usually be obtained from the Court which processed the divorce/dissolution of civil partnership/separation.	*(If the deceased did **not** leave a will, please enclose official copy✦ of the Decree Absolute/Decree of Dissolution of Civil Partnership/Decree of Judicial Separation (as applicable))*	
*D10 Was the deceased legally adopted?	Yes ☐ No ☐	
*D11 Has any relative of the deceased been legally adopted? (If Yes, give name and relationship to deceased.)	Yes ☐ No ☐ Name: Relationship:	

D12 *Answer this section **only** if the deceased died **before 4th April 1988** or left a will or codicil dated before that date.*

D12a Was the deceased illegitimate?	Yes ☐ No ☐	
D12b Did the deceased leave any illegitimate sons or daughters?	Yes ☐ No ☐	
D12c Did the deceased have any illegitimate sons or daughters who died leaving children of their own?	Yes ☐ No ☐	

Important - please complete the checklist overleaf before submitting your application

Important

Checklist

Please return your forms to the probate registry which controls the interview venue at which you wish to be interviewed (see PA4) otherwise your application may be delayed.

Before sending your application, please complete this checklist to confirm that you have enclosed the following items:

1   PA1 (Probate Application Form)   ☐

2   Either IHT205 (signed by all applicants)   ☐
     or IHT421   ☐

     Note: Do not enclose IHT Form 400 — **this must be sent to HMRC (Inheritance Tax) (see PA2)**

3   Original will and codicil(s), **not a photocopy**   ☐
     Note: Do **not** remove or attach anything to the will/codicil

4   Official copy of death certificate or coroner's letter, **not a photocopy**   ☐

5   Other documents as requested on PA1 — please specify   ☐

6   Please state number of official copy grants required for use in England and Wales (see PA3)   ☐

7   Please state number of official copy grants required for use **outside** England and Wales (see PA3)   ☐   **For official use only (sealed and certified)**

8   Please state total amount of cheque enclosed for fee (made payable to HMCS) including cost for the number of official copy grants stated in 6 and 7 above.   £

Note: If you do not enclose all the relevant items, your application may be delayed.

PLEASE ENSURE THAT ALL INFORMATION GIVEN IS ACCURATE AND THAT YOU KEEP COPIES OF ALL DOCUMENTS SENT

Official Use Only

Type of grant:

Power reserved to _____ [Name of executor/s]

Will message: with a codicil / and _____ codicils (delete as appropriate)

Limitation _____

Min interest   Yes / No

Life interest   Yes / No

Figures:- DNE / amounts to   Gross: £

                 Net: £   Fee paid: £

Clearing:-

Title:-

Footnote:-

Guidance Notes
for Probate Application Form PA1

These notes will help you to complete the parts of form PA1 marked *

Section A

A1 Please enclose the original will and any codicils with your application (**not** a photocopy).

A6 Please state the names of any executors named in the will who are not applying for the Grant of Probate and show one of the following reasons for this:-

A   The executor died before the deceased.

B   The executor died after the deceased.

C   The executor does not wish to apply for probate now but wishes to reserve the right to act as executor in the future if necessary – this option is referred to as having "power reserved".

D   The executor does not wish to apply for probate at all. This is referred to as "renouncing". It means that they gives up all their rights to act as executor.

E   The executor wants to appoint another person to act as their attorney to take the Grant of Representation out on their behalf. Please note, however, that the attorney of one executor cannot take a grant jointly with an executor acting in his own right.

If you give reason D or E, please send a letter signed by the executor stating their intention when you send the application to the Probate Registry. If option C, D, or E is stated the Probate Registry will, on receipt of your application, send you a form for the executor(s) to sign to confirm their intention. You should arrange for this to be completed and then return it to the Probate Registry as instructed.

Example for A6

A will appoints three executors – Brian Jones, Valerie Jones and Frank Smith. Brian Jones wishes to apply for the grant, Frank Smith dies before the deceased and Valerie Jones does not wish to apply for the grant at present, as she works full time and cannot attend the appointment. Valerie wishes to keep her options open however, just in case it becomes necessary for her to take out a Grant of Probate in future e.g. if Brian Jones dies before he has completed the administration. The form would be completed as follows:

Frank Smith	**A**
Valerie Jones	**C**

The Grant of Probate will issue to Brian Jones with "power reserved" to Valerie Jones. Valerie Jones will be asked to sign a "power reserved" form.

Section B

Sections B1 - B4 must be completed in all cases. Sections B5 - B6 only needs to be completed if the deceased had no relatives in Sections B1 - B4.

Note:

- This section refers to blood/legally adopted relatives only; details of step relatives are not required.
- The term "survived" means the person was alive when the deceased died.
- If the deceased had any half brothers or sisters/uncles/aunts (i.e. only one parent in common), please indicate this on the form.
- A civil partnership is defined as one between two people of the same sex which has been registered in accordance with the Civil Partnership Act 2004.

B2(c), B4(c) and B6(c)

B2(c) – Only include children of sons or daughters of the deceased entered in B2(b), where the children have survived the deceased.

B4(c) – Only include children of brothers or sisters of the deceased entered in B4(b), where the children have survived the deceased.

B6(c) – Only include children of uncles or aunts of the deceased entered in B6(b), where the children have survived the deceased.

If you are applying on behalf of the person entitled to the grant (i.e. as their attorney), you should send a letter signed by them confirming that they want you to apply with your application. If the person entitled to the grant has already signed an Enduring Power of Attorney (EPA), or a Property and financial affairs Lasting Power of Attorney (LPA) please send the original document to us. An LPA must be registered with the Office of the Public Guardian before it can be used. If the donor of the EPA or LPA is unable to make a decision for him/herself due to an impairment of or a disturbance in the functioning of the mind or brain (i.e. lacks capacity under the Mental Capacity Act (MCA) 2005) please contact us.

Section D

D1 - D2 Please state the full **true** name of the deceased. The true name usually consists of the forenames as shown on the person's birth certificate and the surname as shown on the death certificate. If this is not the case please contact us.

D3 - D4 If the deceased had any assets in any name(s) other than their true name these should be stated. You do not need to show here any assets held jointly with another person.

Example for D1 - D4:

Name on birth certificate	Emma Louise **Jones**
Name on death certificate	Emma Louise **Smith**

The deceased's true name is Emma Louise Smith.

The deceased had a bank account in the name of Louise Smith and was commonly known by this name. The form should be completed as follows:

Forenames	**Emma Louise**
Surname	Smith
Did the deceased hold any assets (excluding joint assets) in another name?	Yes
If yes, what are the assets?	Lloyds Bank Account
And in what name(s) are they held?	**Louise** Smith

The grant will issue in the name of "Emma Louise Smith otherwise known as Louise Smith".

D8 The domicile of the deceased at the date of their death must be established in each case. Generally a person is domiciled in the country which they consider to be their permanent home. However they may be domiciled in a country without having a permanent home there. If you are unsure what this means you should contact your local registry. You may need to seek legal advice regarding this.

D9 You do not initially need to supply a copy of the Decree Absolute, decree of dissolution of civil partnership or decree of Judicial Separation if the deceased left a will. However we may ask to see it later if necessary. You can obtain an official copy of these documents from the court that issued them or from Principal Registry of the Family Division, 42-49 High Holborn, London WC1V 6NP.

D10 - D11 If the deceased did **not** leave a will and the applicant for the grant is the adoptor/adoptee of the deceased, please file a copy of the entry in the Adopted Children's Register. An official copy of the entry in the Adopted Children's Register can be obtained from The General Register Office, Adoption Section, Smedley Hydro, Trafalgar Road, Birkdale, Southport PR8 2HH.

**If you have any general enquiries,
please telephone the Probate and Inheritance Tax Helpline
Telephone number: 0845 3020900**

Application for a probate search

When completing your form please use CAPITAL LETTERS

Details of the Deceased

Surname

Forenames

Probate details (if known)

Grant type: Issuing Registry: Grant issue date:

Date of death/search period*

Address

* (see Conditions of Service
on next page)

Document requirements/payment

Do you want a copy of the Will (if any)?   Yes ☐   No ☐   If Yes, how many? ☐

Do you want a copy of the Grant of Probate
or Letters of Administration (if any)?   Yes ☐   No ☐   If Yes, how many? ☐

I enclose a crossed cheque/Postal Order
(payable to HM Courts Service) to the value of   (see notes on fees
on next page)   £

Your own details

Name/Organisation

Your ref. (if any)

Address/DX number and
Exchange

Please send the completed form, together with your payment, by post to: The Postal Searches and Copies
Department, The Probate Registry, Castle Chambers, Clifford Street, York YO1 9RG (DX720629 York 21)

For official use

Postal Searches and Copies Department: Information and Conditions of Service

Applicable dates and records held: The Postal Searches and Copies Department has indexes relating to all Probate records for the whole of England and Wales from 11 January 1858 up to the present day. You may apply for a copy of any proved Will, as well as a copy of the Grant of Representation. The Grant will tell you who were the Executors or Administrators (those appointed to gather in and distribute the estate). It may also tell you the name of the Solicitor acting for them (if any) and the value of the estate, although usually only in very broad terms. The financial summary shown on the Grant is unfortunately the only information relating to the estate that the Probate record contains. No inventory or estate accounts are available. Occasionally, further details are available from the Capital Taxes Office, but you will normally need the written consent of the executors or administrators. **Please note that, if Probate has not been granted, the Probate Service will have no record of the estate and will therefore not be able to provide copies of any document relating to it.**

If the death was recent, it may be that Probate has not yet been cleared. The Probate procedure itself normally takes some weeks, and there may have been a considerable further delay before the application for Probate was made. Consequently, it may be advisable to wait two or three months after the date of death before having a search made, in order to allow time for the Probate process to be completed.

If you apply before Probate has been completed, you will be notified that no details are available. If you wish to pursue your enquiry, you will need to reapply after a suitable interval, enclosing a further fee and resubmitting all the relevant details, or enter a Standing Search. A Standing Search remains in force for a period of 6 months from the date of entry and provides copies of the Will (if any) and Grant if a Grant issues during this period. Contact the Postal Searches and Copies Department or any Probate Registry for further details.

Other parts of the UK and the Republic of Ireland: The jurisdiction of the Probate Service is limited to England and Wales. If the deceased died domiciled in Scotland, you could try contacting HM Commissary Office, 27 Chambers Street, Edinburgh EH1 2NS (Tel: 0131 247 2850) if the death occurred after 1985, or the Scottish Records Office, HM General Register House, Edinburgh EH1 3YY (Tel: 0131 535 1334) for records prior to this. For Northern Ireland, contact the Probate and Matrimonial Office, The Royal Courts of Justice, Belfast BT1 3JF (Tel: 028 9023 5111), or, if the death occurred more than 7 years ago, the Public Record Office of Northern Ireland, 66 Balmoral Street, Belfast, BT9 6NY (Tel: 028 9025 1318). For the Republic of Ireland, contact the Probate Office, Fourt Courts, Dublin 7 (Tel: Dublin 725555), or the National Archives Office, Bishop Street, Dublin 8 (Tel: Dublin 407 2300) for records more than 20 years old. The Channel Islands and the Isle of Man also have independent Probate Courts.

Fees: When returning the completed application to the Postal Searches and Copies Department in York, please also enclose the fee of £5.00. Each **extra copy** of the same document ordered at the same time will attract an additional fee of £1.00. Cheques or Postal Orders should be crossed and made payable to 'HM Courts Service'. Fees from abroad should be paid by International Money Order, cheque or draft, payable through a United Kingdom bank, and must be made out in £ sterling. We are currently unable to accept payments by credit or debit card, nor are we able to receive search requests by telephone. Please contact the Postal Searches and Copies Department for details of fees for special copies (for instance if you are administering estate abroad), and mark your application accordingly.

The standard fee covers a 4-year search starting from the year in which the death occurred (or the year from which you ask us to start searching). Longer searches are charged at a rate of £3.00 per 4-year period, so that an 8-year search will cost £8.00, and a 12-year search £11.00. Please specify the period to be searched (as well as the date of death if known) and send the appropriate fee. If the death occurred within the last 4 years, the search will be made up to the most recent index. If the search is successful, we will obtain and forward copies of the Will and/or Grant as requested. If no Grant has issued in this time, you will be notified accordingly. We aim to respond to your request within 21 working days.

If a record is traced, the standard fee includes one copy of the Will, if any, and Grant, if requested. Please state clearly which document(s) you require. If the details you supply are incomplete, ambiguous or incorrect and the documents cannot be traced as a result, you will be asked to reapply, giving the correct information and enclosing a further payment. We cannot accept responsibility for the accuracy of the search unless full and correct details are given that accord with the information supplied on application for the Grant, normally the information in the Register of Deaths. If there is insufficient information to make a search, we will contact you for further details. **Please note that your payment is not refundable in the event of a negative search result.**

Original documents: If you are applying for copies of older documents, you should be aware that some of these are in poor condition. Although we make every effort to produce a legible copy from the documents we hold, a small proportion will be of unavoidable poor quality. Furthermore, copies are normally made from the record copies held by the Probate Service. This means that documents prior to the early 1930s will be, by default, copies of manuscript or typescript record copies, and not facsimile copies of the original document. If you want facsimile copies of the original, you will need to mark your request very clearly to that effect.

How to obtain probate -

A guide for people acting without a solicitor

What is the Probate Service?

The Probate Service is part of HMCS. It administers the system of probate, which gives people the legal right to handle the estate (for example, money, possessions and property) of a deceased person.

This leaflet will advise you if you want to obtain probate without using a solicitor.

If you have any queries, please contact your local probate registry. The staff are there to help you – but please note that they cannot give you legal advice.

Introduction

When a person dies, they usually leave an estate (including money, possessions and property) and sometimes a will.

A will should name one or more executors who are responsible for collecting in all the money, paying any debts and distributing any legacies left to individuals or organisations.

In order to access the estate, the executor needs to apply to the probate registry for a document called a Grant of Representation or 'grant'. This process is called probate. The grant establishes who can legally collect money from banks, building societies and other organisations which hold assets belonging to the deceased person.

In most cases, applying for probate is a straightforward procedure. The Probate Service administers applications for grants throughout England and Wales.

The information in this leaflet refers only to the law in England and Wales. If the deceased person was permanently resident in Scotland, Northern Ireland or another country when they died, please contact your nearest probate registry for advice.

What is the purpose of the Grant of Representation?

A Grant of Representation establishes who can legally collect money from banks, building societies and other organisations that hold assets belonging to the deceased person. There are three types of Grant of Representation:

Probate
Probate is issued by the Probate Service to the executor(s) named in the deceased person's will.

Letters of Administration (with will)
Letters of Administration (with will) are issued when no executor is named in the will, or when the executors are unable or unwilling to apply for the grant.

Letters of Administration

Letters of Administration are issued when the deceased person has not made a will, or the will they have made is not valid.

Is a grant always needed?

Not every estate needs a grant. A grant may not be needed if:

- the home is held in joint names and is passing by survivorship to the other joint owner(s). This can be the case for married couples and those in a legal civil partnership.
- there is a joint bank or building society account. In this case, the bank may only need to see the death certificate, in order to arrange for the money to be transferred to the other joint owner. However, a grant could still be needed to access assets held in other bank accounts or insurance policies.
- the amount held in each account was very small. You will need to check with the organisations (banks, building societies or insurance companies) involved to find out if they will release the assets without a grant.

If none of the circumstances above apply, a grant may be required.

You should ask anyone holding the deceased's money (such as a bank or insurance company) whether they will release it to you without seeing a grant. If they agree, they may attach conditions such as asking you to sign a statutory declaration before a solicitor. You can decide whether it is cheaper or easier to do this than to apply for a grant.

Please note that a grant **must** be presented in order to sell or transfer a property held in the deceased's sole name or a share of a property held jointly with the deceased person's spouse or partner as tenants-in-common. Tenancy-in-common is a written agreement between two people who own a joint asset (usually land or buildings). Normally, a married couple does not have a tenancy-in-common contract. If you aren't sure about this, you should consult a solicitor.

You cannot complete a sale on any property owned by a deceased person until the grant has been issued. Properties named in a will should not be put up for sale until a grant has been obtained.

Who can apply for probate?

It isn't necessary for everyone left money or property in a will to apply for probate. Usually, only one person needs to do it – normally the executor(s) named in the will.

However, if the person entitled to the estate is under 18, two people are legally required to apply for probate. If this is the case we will let you know when we receive your application.

You can apply for probate if you are over the age of 18 and:

- you are an executor named in the will;
- you are named in the will to receive some or all of the estate (if there are no executors, or if the executors are unable or unwilling to apply);

- the deceased person did not make a will and you are their next of kin, in the following order of priority:

  - lawful husband or wife or civil partner (a civil partnership is defined as a partnership between two people of the same sex which has been registered in accordance with the Civil Partnership Act 2004). Common law partners cannot apply for probate.

  - sons or daughters (excluding step-children) including children adopted by the deceased. (Children adopted out of the family can only apply in the estates of their adoptive parents and not their biological parents.)

  - parents

  - brothers or sisters

  - grandparents

  - uncles or aunts

  - If sons, daughters, brothers, sisters, uncles or aunts of the deceased person have died before the deceased, their children may apply for probate.

If you are not sure whether you are entitled to apply for a grant, you should still complete and return the forms and we will tell you. If you are a distant relative, please supply a brief family tree showing your relationship to the deceased person.

When more than one person wants to apply for a grant, they may make a joint application. A maximum of four applicants is allowed and they will all have to attend an interview with the Probate Service.

Where will I find the will?

The original will may be held at a solicitor's office or bank, or at the Principal Probate Registry in London. It may be among the deceased person's possessions. If you cannot find it, contact your local Probate Registry. If you do not send the will, your application will take longer to deal with.

We will not return the original will to you as it becomes a public record once it has been proved (acted on). We will, however, send you an official copy of the will with the Grant of Representation.

What if I don't want to apply for a grant?

Executors may choose to give up all their rights to probate or they may reserve the right, called power reserved, to apply for probate in the future.

This option is often used when the executors live in different parts of the country or it is not convenient for one of them to attend the interview due to work commitments.

Only the executor(s) who attend the interview will be named on the grant and only their signature will be required to release the deceased person's assets for transfer or sale.

If the person who is entitled to the grant does not wish to apply, they may appoint someone else to be their attorney to obtain the grant on their behalf. If this is the case you should complete their details on form **PA1** (Section C). We will send you a form for them to sign after we receive your application. If the person entitled to the grant has already signed an Enduring Power of Attorney (EPA) or a Lasting Power of Attorney (LPA) please file the original document with your application.

Note – A LPA must be registered with the Office of the Public Guardianship before it can be used.

You can contact them at: www.publicguardian.gov.uk or by calling 0845 330 2900.

Why do I need to think about Inheritance Tax now?

The tax on the estate of a person who has died is called Inheritance Tax. It is dealt with by HM Revenue & Customs (HMRC) (Inheritance Tax). It only applies to a very small percentage of estates. If Inheritance Tax is due, you normally have to pay at least some of the tax before we can issue the grant.

The issue of the grant does not mean that HMRC (Inheritance Tax) have agreed the final Inheritance Tax liability. They will usually contact you again after you have received the grant. Subject to the requirements to pay some of the tax before obtaining the grant, Inheritance Tax is due six months after the end of the month in which the person died. HMRC (Inheritance Tax) will charge interest on unpaid tax from this due date whatever the reason for late payment.

Probate Registry staff are not trained to deal with queries about HMRC forms or Inheritance Tax. If you have any queries about these you should visit the HMRC website: www.hmrc.gov.uk/inheritancetax/ or contact the Probate and Inheritance Tax Helpline on 0845 30 20 900.

How do I apply for a grant?

You will need to follow the process explained here:

Complete the application form

You will need to complete **Probate Application form PA1, using Guidance Leaflet PA1A**. You can also get these forms from your nearest probate registry or by calling the Probate and Inheritance Tax Helpline – see page 7 for details.

These documents can also be downloaded from our website (www.hmcourts-service.gov.uk) where you should print off a blank **PA1** and then complete it by hand.

On the application form, you should tell us which Probate Registry interview venue you would like to visit – you can choose the one which is most convenient for you, and any other executors.

Complete the tax form

When you apply for the grant, you will need to complete a tax form **whether or not Inheritance Tax is owed**. You should use form **IHT205** if no Inheritance Tax is owed. If form **IHT205** is not applicable to you, please contact HMRC (Inheritance Tax) for form **IHT400**.

For help completing the forms, you can contact the Probate and Inheritance Tax Helpline (the phone number is on page 7 of this leaflet). You can either work out the Inheritance Tax for yourself or you can ask HMRC to do it for you.

Decide how many official sealed copies of the Grant of Representation you need

Organisations like banks and building societies need to see sealed copies of the grant before they can release assets to you. They won't accept unsealed photocopies.

So if you want to deal with the estate quickly, you may want to order enough sealed copies of the grant to send to all the organisations you are dealing with at the same time.

If there are any assets held outside England and Wales, you may require a special copy of the grant – usually referred to as a sealed and certified copy.

If any person or organisation holding assets insists on seeing an official copy of the grant, you can write to the probate registry, which issued the grant to order more sealed copies. However, these will cost more than those ordered at the time of application (see the fee list), so it's important to decide before you apply for the grant how many copies you will need.

Make sure you enclose the correct documents

You will need to enclose:

- An official copy (not a photocopy) of the death certificate issued by the Registrar of Births Deaths and Marriages or a coroner's certificate.
- The **original** will and any codicils (or any document in which the deceased person expresses any wishes about the distribution of his or her estate). Keep a copy of any will or codicil you send us. Please do not attach anything to the will by staple, pin etc. or remove any fastenings from the will.
- Any other documents specifically requested by the Probate Service, such as a decree absolute.
- A cheque made payable to 'HMCS' for the application fee, together with the cost of the number of official sealed grants you require. See the fees list on form **PA3**. (We cannot process your application until the fee has been paid.)

Where should I send my application?

You should send your application to the probate registry of your choice (see the enclosed leaflet **PA4** for the address). You may wish to send your application by registered or recorded post.

Processing the application

When we receive your application, we will examine it and contact you if there are any queries. If you want us to acknowledge your application, please send a stamped addressed envelope.

If your application is complicated, we may require you to sign additional documents or contact other people – for example, a witness to a will – so that we can interview them or obtain their signatures on documents to help with your application.

If there are no problems, we will send you a letter (usually 10 days after we receive your application) inviting you to a 10-15 minute interview at the location you have chosen. This interview is usually held within a month of receiving your application.

If you are applying for a grant with someone else and they cannot come with you, we can arrange for them to attend an interview separately at a different location if necessary. This will, however, delay the time it takes to issue your grant.

What happens at the interview?

The interview is simply to confirm the details you have given on the forms and to answer any queries you or we may have.

We also ask you to sign a form of oath and to swear or affirm before the interviewing officer that the information you have given is true to the best of your knowledge. You will be given the opportunity to swear on the religious book of your choice.

Please bring proof of identification which includes a photograph (such as your driving licence or passport) to the interview. Your appointment letter will tell you about any other identification which is required.

The interview is your chance to tell the interviewing officer if your case is urgent or if you wish to collect the grant in person.

What happens after the interview?

If everything goes smoothly, we will send you the original grant and copies of the grant (if you have requested them) and the original death certificate. The interviewing officer should be able to let you know how long this will take.

If it is not possible to issue a grant, we will explain the reasons.

We retain the original will, as it becomes a public record.

How do I use the grant?

When the grant has been issued you will receive information concerning your role as the executor. You will then have the legal right to ask any person or organisation holding the deceased person's money or property to give you access to these assets. These assets can then be released, sold or transferred as set out in the deceased person's will.

All grants of representation are public records.

The responsibility of the Probate Service ends when the grant is issued, and we cannot advise you on how to administer the estate. If you have any questions about this, you should seek legal advice.

Useful contacts

For general information on wills and probate:
www.direct.gov.uk/en/RightsAndResponsibilities/Death/index.htm

For information about the Probate Service and to access the online forms and leaflets:
http://www.hmcourts-service.gov.uk/infoabout/civil/probate/index.htm

To find the addresses of the regional probate registries:
http://www.hmcourts-service.gov.uk/infoabout/civil/probate/registries.htm

For information about Inheritance Tax and online forms:
www.hmrc.gov.uk/inheritancetax/

For more detailed information about probate and Inheritance Tax:
Probate and Inheritance Tax Helpline: 0845 3020900

Probate forms and leaflets

PA1   Probate application form

PA1A   Probate application form (guidance notes)

PA2   How to obtain probate (leaflet)

PA3   Probate fees list (leaflet)

PA4   Directory of probate registries and interview venues (leaflet)

PA5   Do I need a grant of representation (probate or letters of administration)? (leaflet)

PA6   What will happen at my probate interview? (leaflet)

PA7   How to deposit a will with the Probate Service (leaflet)

PA7A   Withdrawing your will from the Principal Probate Registry (form)

PA8   How to enter a caveat (leaflet)

PA8A   How to enter a caveat (form)

PA9   How to enter a general search (leaflet)

PA10   How to enter a standing search (leaflet)

PA1S   Application for a probate search (form)

HMRC Inheritance Tax forms

IHT205 Return of estate information

IHT206 Return of estate information (guidance notes)

IHT400 Inheritance Tax Account

Probate Fees

	Fee
Application In all cases where the net estate (ie the amount remaining in the deceased's sole name after funeral expenses and debts owing have been deducted) is **over £5,000** (see example 1 below). **Note: Joint assets passing automatically to the surviving joint owner should not be included when calculating the fee.**	£90
If the net estate as above is **under £5,000** (see example 2 below).	No fee
Application for a second grant in an estate where a previous grant has been issued.	£15
Additional Copies Official (sealed) copies of the Grant of Representation if ordered when you lodge your application for a Grant of Representation. **Note: You should decide how many copies you will need and add the cost to your application fee – this will give you the total amount payable. See examples below. It can save you a lot of time when collecting in the deceased's assets if you have a few extra copies of the grant to produce to the organisations holding the assets.**	£1 per copy
'Sealed and certified copy' – if assets are held abroad you may need one of these. Please check with the appropriate organisations before ordering.	£1 per copy (including Will and Grant)
Additional copies (consisting of grant including a copy of the Will, if applicable) ordered after the Grant of Representation has been issued.	£5 for first copy then £1 per additional copy

Example 1				**Example 2**			
Net estate of £75,000	=	Fee	£90	Net estate of £2,000	=	Fee	Nil
4 copies of grant at £1	=	Fee	£ 4	1 copy of grant at £1	=	Fee	£1
each		Total Fee	£94	each		Total Fee	£1

Please send a cheque or postal order (no cash) made payable to "**HM Courts Service**", together with your application forms, to the Probate Registry to which you are applying. You should state the number and type of copies you need on the checklist on page 4 of the PA1 (application form). Please print the name of the **deceased person** on the back of the cheque.

Please ensure you order sufficient copies for your needs, when you send in your application.

Please note: Appropriate post must be paid. (Standard rate postage may not be sufficient. If your forms weigh over 60g they may need to be weighed at your local Post Office.)

Fee Refunds/Remissions

If you consider that you would suffer financial hardship if you pay a court fee you can apply for remission (or if you have already paid a fee a refund of that fee or part thereof). If you wish to make such an application you should ask a member of the Registry staff to supply you with form EX160 (including form EX160A). Please note that fee exemption, as described in that booklet, does not apply with regard to non-contentious probate fees.

Your application will not be processed until the fee is paid (or an application for refund/remission has been successful).

(04.07)

Directory of Probate Registries and Interview Venues

> **For general enquiries, please telephone the Probate & Inheritance Tax Help-line Monday to Friday 9.00 to 5.00 on 0845 3020900.**
>
> **For enquiries about appointments, or for enquiries after you have sent your forms to a Probate Registry, please contact the Registry concerned, using the number listed below.**

Controlling Probate Registries (except Carlisle, Chester, Lancaster, London and Middlesbrough) are open to the public 9.30am to 4.00pm Monday-Friday.

You can choose any venue for your interview appointment, **but your application forms *must* be sent to the Controlling Probate Registry responsible for that venue.**

Interview locations, other than Probate Registries, have limited opening times. When selecting such a venue your interview will be fixed for the next available date. If, when you receive notification of that date, you require an earlier interview, you should telephone the controlling Registry (phone number will be supplied at that time) to see if an earlier date at the controlling Registry can be arranged.

Controlling Probate Registry	Interview Venues	Controlling Probate Registry	Interview Venues
Birmingham District Probate Registry The Priory Courts 33 Bull Street Birmingham B4 6DU Tel: 0121 681 3400/3414	Birmingham Coventry Kidderminster Northampton Wolverhampton	**Carlisle Probate Sub-Registry** Courts of Justice Earl Street, Carlisle CA1 1DJ Tel: 01228 521751	Carlisle
Bodmin Probate Sub-Registry Bodmin Magistrates Court Launceston Road Bodmin Cornwall PL31 2AL Tel: 01208 261581	Bodmin Plymouth Truro	**Carmarthen Probate Sub-Registry** 14 King Street Carmarthen SA31 1BL Tel: 01267 242560	Carmarthen Aberystwyth Haverfordwest Swansea
Brighton District Probate Registry William Street Brighton BN2 0RF Tel: 01273 573510	Brighton Chichester Hastings Horsham	**Chester Probate Sub-Registry** Please send applications to Liverpool District Probate Registry (see address on page 2)	
Bristol District Probate Registry Ground Floor The Crescent Centre Temple Back Bristol BS1 6EP Tel: 0117 927 3915/926 4619	Bristol Bath Weston-Super-Mare	**Exeter Probate Sub-Registry** 1st Floor Exeter Crown & County Courts Southernhay Gardens Exeter, Devon EX1 1UH Tel: 01392 415370	Exeter Barnstaple Taunton Torquay/Newton Abbot Yeovil
Caernarfon Probate Sub-Registry The Criminal Justice Centre Llanberis Road Caernarfon LL55 2DF Tel: 01286 669 755	Caernarfon Rhyl Wrexham	**Gloucester Probate Sub-Registry** 2nd Floor, Combined Court Building Kimbrose Way Gloucester GL1 2DG Tel: 01452 834966	Gloucester Cheltenham Hereford Worcester
Cardiff Probate Registry of Wales 3rd Floor, Cardiff Magistrates' Court Fitzalan Place, Cardiff South Wales CF24 0RZ Tel: 02920 474373	Cardiff Bridgend Newport Pontypridd	**Ipswich District Probate Registry** Ground Floor 8 Arcade Street Ipswich IP1 1EJ Tel: 01473 284260	Ipswich Chelmsford Colchester

Controlling Probate Registry	Interview Venues	Controlling Probate Registry	Interview Venues
Lancaster Probate Sub-Registry Please send applications to Liverpool District Probate Registry (see address below)		**Newcastle-Upon-Tyne District Probate Registry** Newcastle DPR No 1 Waterloo Square Newcastle-Upon-Tyne NE1 4DR Tel: 0191 211 2170	Newcastle-Upon-Tyne Darlington Middlesbrough
Leeds District Probate Registry 3rd Floor, Coronet House Queen Street Leeds LS1 2BA Tel: 0113 386 3540	Leeds	**Norwich Probate Sub-Registry** Combined Court Building The Law Courts Bishopgate Norwich NR3 1UR Tel: 01603 728267	Norwich Kings Lynn Lowestoft
Leicester Probate Sub-Registry Crown Court Building 90 Wellington Street Leicester LE1 6HG Tel: 0116 285 3380	Leicester Bedford	**Nottingham Probate Sub-Registry** Butt Dyke House 33 Park Row Nottingham NG1 6GR Tel: 0115 941 4288	Nottingham
Lincoln Probate Sub-Registry 360 High Street Lincoln LN5 7PS Tel: 01522 523648	Lincoln	**Oxford District Probate Registry** Combined Court Building St Aldates Oxford OX1 1TL Tel: 01865 793055	Oxford Aylesbury High Wycombe Reading Slough Swindon
Liverpool District Probate Registry The Queen Elizabeth II Law Courts Derby Square Liverpool L2 1XA Tel: 0151 236 8264	Liverpool Southport Lancaster Blackpool Preston St Helens Chester	**Peterborough Probate Sub-Registry** 1st Floor, Crown Building Rivergate Peterborough PE1 1EJ Tel: 01733 562802	Peterborough Cambridge
London Probate Department Principal Registry of the Family Division First Avenue House 42-49 High Holborn London WC1V 6NP Tel: 020 7947 6939 Open 10.00am-4.30pm Mon-Fri	London Croydon Edmonton Harlow Kingston Luton Southend-on-Sea Woolwich	**Sheffield Probate Sub-Registry** PO Box 832 The Law Courts 50 West Bar Sheffield S3 8YR Tel: 0114 281 2596	Sheffield
Maidstone Probate Sub-Registry The Law Courts Barker Road Maidstone ME16 8EQ Tel: 01622 202048	Maidstone Canterbury Tunbridge Wells	**Stoke-on-Trent Probate Sub-Registry** Combined Court Centre Bethesda Street Hanley Stoke-on-Trent ST1 3BP Tel: 01782 854065	Stoke-on-Trent Stafford Shrewsbury Crewe
Manchester District Probate Registry Manchester Civil Justice Centre Ground Floor 1 Bridge Street West PO Box 4240 Manchester M60 1WJ Tel: 0161 240 5700	Manchester Bolton Burnley Oldham Warrington Wigan	**Winchester District Probate Registry** 4th Floor Cromwell House Andover Road Winchester SO23 7EW Tel: 01962 897029	Winchester Basingstoke Bournemouth Dorchester Guildford Newport I.O.W. Portsmouth Salisbury Southampton
Middlesbrough Probate Sub-Registry Please send applications to Newcastle District Probate Registry (see address opposite)		**York Probate Sub-Registry** 1st Floor Castle Chambers Clifford Street York YO1 9RG Tel: 01904 666777	York Hull Scarborough

What will happen at my probate interview?

A guide for people seeking to obtain probate

What is the Probate Service?

The Probate Service is part of HMCS. It administers the system of probate, which gives people the legal right to handle the estate (for example, money, possessions and property) of a deceased person.

This leaflet is to tell you what to expect if you are going to attend a probate interview.

If you have any queries, please contact your local probate registry. The staff are there to help you – but they cannot give you legal advice.

Introduction

When a person dies, they usually leave an estate (including money, possessions and property) and sometimes a will.

Any will names one or more executors to be responsible for collecting in all the money, paying any debts and distributing any legacies left to individuals or organisations.

In order to access the estate, the executor needs to apply to the probate registry for a document called a Grant of Representation or 'grant'. This process is called probate.

In most cases, applying for probate is a straightforward procedure. The probate registry administers applications for grants throughout England and Wales.

Why do I need to come for an interview?

The interview is to confirm the information that you have provided in your application for probate, so that we can issue a Grant of Representation to you. The interview will also give you the opportunity to ask any questions you may have.

Where will the interview take place?

The interview will be held at the venue given on your appointment letter. This should be the venue you requested when you filled in the application form. If this isn't correct, please contact the probate registry you sent your application to, before the date of the interview. The appointment will be in a private room. You will not have to go into a courtroom.

Please follow the instructions on your appointment letter and ensure you arrive 10 minutes before your interview, so that you don't cause any delay.

Who is the interview with?

The interview will be informal. You will meet a member of staff from the Probate Service called a Commissioner. You will not have to see a judge.

What facilities will be available?

Please see your appointment letter for specific details. If you have any special needs, please contact the probate registry you sent your application to, before the date of the interview.

Can I bring a friend or relative with me?

Yes, you are welcome to do so.

Do I need to bring any identification with me?

Yes – each applicant for the Grant of Representation should bring two separate forms of identification (one of which should include a photograph of you) from the following list:

- full driving licence;
- passport;
- official bus pass;
- National Identity Card/Identification Card/Identity Card for Foreign Nationals;
- National Insurance card;
- National Health card;
- State Pension notification letter;
- Child Benefit notification letter;
- a letter or invoice from a utilities company showing your current address; or
- a council tax bill.

If you do not have any of these forms of identification please contact us before your interview.

What else do I need to bring?

If we have asked you to bring any documents with you to the interview, please don't forget them or your interview may have to be rearranged for another day.

If you wear glasses for reading, please remember to bring them.

What will happen at the interview?

The interview should take no longer than 15 minutes. You will be asked to read through a document called 'The Oath', which we will have prepared from the information you gave us in your application form.

You will then be asked to confirm that the information in the document is correct to the best of your knowledge.

Next, you will be asked to swear on the religious book of your choice that the information in the document is correct.

If you do not want to swear on the New Testament, you can choose one of these two alternatives:

- make an affirmation (which means to make a legal declaration that the information on your application is correct);
- swear on another religious book. If you want to use an alternative religious book, please contact the office named on your appointment letter before the day of the interview.

Remember that if you wilfully make a statement which you know to be false or do not believe to be true or knowingly withhold information, you could be prosecuted.

Will I be given the grant at the interview?

No, it will be posted to you, usually within 10 working days of your interview – together with any copies you have paid for.

If your grant is urgent or you wish to collect it in person, please tell the interviewing officer.

If you have completed **Tax Form IHT421** for HM Revenue & Customs (HMRC), the grant and copies will be posted to you once HMRC (Inheritance Tax) has confirmed that it is satisfied that the Grant of Representation can be issued.

If you have questions about Inheritance Tax, please call the Probate and Inheritance Tax Helpline – you'll find the number at the back of this leaflet.

Which documents will I get back?

The death certificate will be returned to you with the grant. However, the original will is not returned to you, as it becomes a public record. You will receive an official copy of the will with the Grant of Representation.

Useful contacts

For general information on wills and probate:
www.direct.gov.uk/en/RightsAndResponsibilities/Death/index.htm

For information about the Probate Service and online forms:
http://www.hmcourts-service.gov.uk/infoabout/civil/probate/index.htm

To find out addresses of regional probate registries:
http://www.hmcourts-service.gov.uk/infoabout/civil/probate/registries.htm

For information about Inheritance Tax and online forms:
www.hmrc.gov.uk/inheritancetax/

For more detailed information about probate and Inheritance Tax:
Probate and Inheritance Tax Helpline: 0845 3020900

Probate forms and leaflets

PA1   Probate application form

PA1A   Probate application form (guidance notes)

PA2   How to obtain probate (leaflet)

PA3   Probate fees list (leaflet)

PA4   Directory of probate registries and interview venues (leaflet)

PA5   Do I need a grant of representation (probate or letters of administration)? (leaflet)

PA6   What will happen at my probate interview? (leaflet)

PA7   How to deposit a will with the Probate Service (leaflet)

PA7A   Withdrawing your will from the Principal Probate Registry (form)

PA8   How to enter a caveat (leaflet)

PA8A   How to enter a caveat (form)

PA9   How to enter a general search (leaflet)

PA10   How to enter a standing search (leaflet)

PA1S   Application for a probate search (form)

PA6 What will happen at my probate interview? (11.09)

© Crown copyright 2009

Page 4

Index